His Song I Sing

Jean Varlese

Trafford rev. 09/14/2018

 www.trafford.com
North America & international
toll-free: 1 888 232 4444 (USA & Canada)
fax: 812 355 4082

In Memory of

Anthony Varlese Jr.

February 9, 1962 - November 27, 1997

DEDICATION

This book is dedicated to all those

victimized by the

"Silent Epidemic"

and

To the surviving families

who had to endure the

aftermath of this tragedy

Table of Contents

PREFACE

How does one venture into the most profound recount of a very sad, unexplainable turn of events, of a life that had a most perfect beginning but culminated in a deadly end? There are no words humanly possible to expound the inner feelings of a loss so great that makes one question the existence of oneself, after this loss has taken hold of your intellect, your reasoning and most of all the unending questioning of the fate that befell an individual so dear, so important, that the intricate facets of your own life and existence leaves you with no meaning or purpose. How does one go on? Where does one find peace? Where do the answers come from? If ever, are there any answers?

The loss of a child is the most devastating tragedy to be endured by any parent. It is not the normal course of life to have to inter your offspring. With this said, the purpose of writing this biographical synopsis of my son's short lived life, is about my son, and *for my son*. This is the most significant method I have to keep him close to me, in thoughts and emotions. He may not have been a rocket scientist, but he was truly a good, decent, respectful, honest human being that existed briefly, and to his family and friends he was a very powerful person. Hopefully this book will capture and express his nature, his kindness and above all his **LOVE** for all his family and friends.

Jean Varlese

ACKNOWLEDGMENTS

First and foremost to my **Husband Tony**, not only for helping with the mechanics and the tedious editing of this biography, but for his patience, strength and endurance in helping me cope with my pain and sadness, even though he likewise grieves for his son.

To my daughter **Gina Maurer**, and her family, **Bob, Andrew and Kerrin**, for having to endure even another sad hurdle in their lives. Gina not only lost her only brother but lost a part of her mother.

To my best friend **Maryann Nicholson**, for always being there for me, especially being a second Mom to Tony for 35 years.

To **Billy Nicholson**, who was not only Tony's best friend, but who also graciously helped us launch Tony's website.

To my friends at *"A Time for Healing"*, a bereavement group for Survivors of Suicide, and *"Compassionate Friends"*, a bereavement group for those who have lost a child. Without their support and encouragement, I am not sure I would have had the strength and courage to function again.

To **Veronica and George Pazolt**, my newly adopted "Sister of Choice", for their friendship, compassion and understanding, and all while sharing their own grief and pain for the loss of their son **Gary**, also to suicide.

To **ALL** my son's friends, who willingly and graciously gave of their time to include their beautiful and precious memories of Tony, throughout this book.

Last but not least, to countless family and friends who throughout my ordeal, held my hand, gave me a shoulder to cry on, listened without criticism and also shed their own tears along with mine.

With thanks and appreciation,   *Jean Varlese*

CHAPTER ONE

PRECIOUS CHILD

> *In my dreams you are alive and well, Precious Child*
> *In my dreams I see you clear as a bell, Precious Child*
> *In my soul there is a hole, that can never be filled*
> *For in my heart there is hope, cause you are with me still.*

Gone, at the age of thirty-five, our precious child. The universal questions of why him? Why us? Always the response to cause and effect. These questions are the outward earthly ones; the real spiritual mystical ones are the hard ones to answer. What was our child suffering from? The investigation revealed nothing strange or foreign, nothing out of the ordinary, nothing to indicate our child was not a normal healthy young man, who could have and would have spent many years giving us the joy, happiness and especially the *love* he had always shown.

The baby, the boy, the teenager, the adult man, nowhere were there any indications that his life should have ended so young, so suddenly, so untimely. A parent searches for explanations when lightning strikes out of the blue, when breath ceases, and icy coldness sets in.

Parents examine their own inner souls, their own inadequacies, and their own inability to have missed something that went awry.

Human instinct is to rear your children, protect them at any cost, teach, guide and allow them to obtain their full potential; this is an innate trait of all parents. At this untimely tragedy, we pondered our own past, looked for mistakes we may have made, searched for signs we may have missed, questioned our own up-bringing, our culture, our ancestry as far back as we could, and found nothing *concrete* that we could possibly latch on to.

Again, questions!, questions!, questions!. Where were all the answers? In our minds, in our hearts, we found none.

This was the end. Here is the beginning:

I was due to deliver my second child on February 22, 1962 (George Washington's Birthday). "How great!", I remarked, my child would share a special day with someone famous. Back in 1962 we did not celebrate "President's Day", therefore, my child would always have a day off from school on his birthday, so I proclaimed. I use the masculine pronoun, not because I had previous knowledge that it would be a boy, only because it was my inner hopes and wishes to have a son. Forty years ago we were not fortunate to have the technology we have today, to be able to know ahead of time the sex of the unborn, nor did I wish to know.

My unborn child had an agenda all his own; he surprised us and arrived two weeks early. He was born on February 9th, which also happened to be the birthday of another president, William Henry Harrison. This president was not as well known as our first president, but notable nonetheless. It is ironic that all of us share a birthday with a president. Tony Sr., with Richard M. Nixon (January 9th), Gina, our daughter, shares her birthday with Franklin D. Roosevelt (January 30th) and I with Benjamin Harrison (August 20th).

Tony, as he wished to be called, instead of Anthony, was born without any prior incident, after a normal pregnancy, and after a normal nine-hour labor. He arrived at 1:00 pm at Astoria General Hospital in Astoria, New York. He weighed in at 8 lbs. and was 21 inches long. He was my perfect boy. I mention this, not because I was biased, but because later in this chapter, I will relate the birth of Tony's sister Gina, whose birth was marred by an emotional course of events.

Our child was born to proud parents, Anthony and Jean and a precious brother to Gina. Tony's delivery, as I mentioned, was a normal one or **so I thought.** On the day we were to be discharged from the hospital, I began to hemorrhage and my physician found it necessary that I return to the operating room to find out what complications had arisen from the delivery. But, before I was taken to the O.R., I clearly remember becoming semi-conscious and fading into a deep dark space. This was due to the loss of blood. As I was falling into this abyss, my only thoughts were of this precious child, whom I had just given birth to, he would be left without a mother to guide him, nurture him, love him and help him grow into maturity. All else and everyone else were in oblivion, my husband, my daughter, my parents; no one else seemed to be in my vision. The only sight I had was of my son, Tony. I felt I was leaving this world and I would not see him again.

There are days, **now,** I sometimes feel God would have been kind to me had this been the case. I was spared then, but certainly not spared today. The black hole I was descending into on February 14, 1962 was postponed to November 28, 1997, the day my husband and I found our only son sitting in his 1997 black Firebird convertible, in the garage of his new house in Nesconset, New York. The home he had purchased only nine weeks prior to this fatal day. A home they acquired with so much care, so much enthusiasm, and so much *Love.* He and his wife had shopped for this dream house for several months, a lot of thought went into the selection, the style, the location, the neighbors they would have, making sure there would be other children, the proximal ages of their own two sons. How sad, how cruel, how very unfortunate that nine weeks later he was gone.

Our baby was a very quiet child, simply feed him, change his diaper, cuddle and coo him and he always returned your attention with the biggest, brightest smile ever. He had no colic, was never cranky, and made no unnecessary demands. How blessed we all felt.

When Tony arrived perfectly *normal*, I thanked God with my entire spiritual acknowledgment and with every fiber of my being. I had already been to Hades and back, torturing myself with blame, guilt and sorrow all rolled into one with the birth of our daughter Gina, that when Tony was born four years later, he became my salvation, mentally and emotionally. I knew God was good to me, first giving me a girl, that in time we were hopeful she would be okay, we would try to regain our dreams and muster up enough will power to carry on and now my second child was born a beautiful baby boy. Emotions were high and expectations for a normal family was within our reach.

My son's personality was 180-degrees out of phase from his sister's. He took everything in stride, quietly, calmly, always accepting his inadequacies, **outwardly at least**. He paled in comparison to his sister, again she being very outgoing, a doer, a leader, a plaintiff, a go-getter no matter what, Gina was certainly exceptional. To retrace my first pregnancy and the birth of Tony's sister Gina, who was born four years earlier on January 30, 1958 and who, due to providence or perhaps a reaction to a prescribed morning sickness drug similar to Thalidomide, which was found to cause birth defects when taken in the early trimester of pregnancy, Gina was born physically challenged. We will not paraphrase the common terminology 'handicapped'. I will embellish and note that Gina was a very demanding baby, not due to her impediment at this time, but simply because she was of the female persuasion and she needed more attention.

Gina was a very spirited, active, spunky baby. Nothing stood in her way, not even her 'so-called' handicap. She was, to say the least, a handful.

When Gina was born, the tears were abundant, the future was dark, I feared for her every minute of every day. As she started to grow, my outlook on life began to get a little more hopeful because she seemed to cope a heck of a lot better than I did at the time. Our families stood a close watch over Gina and me. She, because of her impediment, and me because of my unstable emotional outbursts. They helped with taking care of her and constantly reassuring me things would get better and that life would be brighter. I would always nod, in agreement, so they wouldn't get offended, but I was so pessimistic when it concerned Gina's future. For my family it was a lot easier said than done because they could not possibly imagine what was in my heart, what was on my mind, the deep tortures in my very being. No matter what was said to me, the hurting, aching, future uncertainties, the grim outlook of life was very hard to dismiss. At that time, for me there were no acceptances of the defeats of life, the sadness of the abnormal birth of your first born. My realization and salvation of this challenge was in prayer, that there must be a reason for all this heartache. Not quite acceptable yet was that God needed to keep me within His constant call. Every waking minute I questioned God's reason for this hurt in myself and in my beautiful child. There was always the inner blame that it was I who angered God for whatever reason and so He needed to set me straight. The path God chose was indeed a very long and arduous one.

Gina would never be like other girls; she would always be *different*. Gina required several surgeries as an infant, commencing at age nine months through age thirteen, and always the outcome was never certain. We traveled from one doctor to another in the hopes that someone would give us some positive answers. Would she ever walk? Would she always spend her life in a wheelchair? Would she need crutches? Would she wear braces? So many questions for months, there were no answers. We, after consulting with numerous orthopedic specialists, even traveled to Bologna Italy for a consultation and finally found a doctor in Orange, New Jersey, Dr. Henry Kessler from the Kessler Institute of Rehabilitation. After examining our daughter Dr. Kessler gave us a positive glimmer of hope, somehow he was *certain* she would walk, under what conditions were yet to be determined. When Gina was twenty months old and after two surgeries, she began to walk, now the picture became a little clearer, a little brighter. The challenge was a slight bit less difficult. Gina's attitude was great for a child so young. She certainly taught her mom a few new things. "I will overcome", was not only a similar statement made by Dr. Martin Luther King Jr., but repeated many times by my tiny little girl. Due to her impairment she was a very slight built toddler. Her legs were shorter because of the missing fibulas, and her missing tarsi and metatarsals made her feet small and deformed. She may not have grown in height, but she rapidly grew in wisdom more than anyone could possibly imagine.

After four years of anguish for everyone involved, I began to feel blessed when Tony was born, I felt God had somehow closed a door, but opened a window. I began to see life as a true gift, and so I treasured, through pain, my daughter's aspirations, challenges and eventually her successes at each hurdle, each obstacle, and each achievement even though there were many disappointments placed in her path. I cannot stress enough the anguish encountered by this child throughout her life. Even as an adult today there are numerous times when pain hinders her somewhat in her everyday normal living, but she continues to endure.

I recall, at the tender age of thirteen, Gina was placed in a position where she was burdened with the decision to have her legs amputated. The doctors were suggesting that the implemented prosthesis would allow her to have normal size and normal shaped legs. Could you possibly imagine what a monumental decision this would be for any young child to have to make, and yet here she was placed in this horrendous position. We, as her parents, together with the physician in charge, gave

Gina all the pros and cons that a surgery such as this would entail, the consequences that would ensue, but the ultimate decision should and *had* to be made by her. Gina spent hours pondering and agonizing this decision carefully, calculating every aspect involved, and arrived at a very mature decision of opting to remain with the deformity and limitations with which she was born. Her reasoning was logical and sensible. The glory part, the glamorous part did not phase her, neither was the pain that she would have had to endure from the surgery and its recuperating time. The reason she declined was so simple that not even a very mature adult would have come to such a unique decision.

She felt in times of emergencies she would have to secure her prosthesis first before she could ambulate. With her own legs she could maneuver faster. I will inevitably recount more of Gina's involvement in Tony's life at a later time throughout this writing. How their lives intertwined, how their lives meshed, separately and united, especially in his final days.

My excerpting Gina's infancy and childhood was simply to capture the differences in my children's personalities and in essence in comparing the "angel" (the term used here is explained in Chapter 2) sent to us four years later. I am not implying that Gina was not an angel, I am inferring that she was a handful, both in the physical and emotional capacities. After all, she was a female and females do have a mind of their own. A personality that is unique only to the feminine gender. In Gina's situation it was to her advantage to be headstrong and spunky. She was better able to cope with her physical differences and better able to defend herself from cruel children who did not know how harmful they could be with their snide remarks about her "ugly shoes" her "baby high ankle laced up shoes", her "short legs", etc. Through all of this, there were no problems she would not tackle on her own. There were no challenges she would not attempt. She played sports, sometimes better than most. She played first baseman on the "Blue Jays" girls softball little league team, and actually became one of their better players.

She sang and danced in our school plays, even though she found it difficult since her balancing coordination was impaired. The one thing she did not wish to do was "be different". The one thing she would always try to do was minimize her pain so that we would allow her to participate.

There is a specific time we vividly recall, Gina was a 'Seaman' in the Sea Rangers (an organization comparable to the Girl Scouts of America), and she was requested to march in their annual parade. This parade was approximately four miles in length through the city streets in Rosedale. Her dad walked on the sidelines in case she got tired and needed to dismiss herself from the group. To the astonishment of both us and the Sea Ranger Captain, Gina walked the entire parade on her own, without assistance of any sort. She later received a bronze commendation plaque for her extraordinary efforts, stamina and will power. All of this verified Gina's gutsy personality, her strong character and a maturity beyond her years.

As a toddler, Tony also had times of strong character and bravery for someone so young. It was at the age of three, my husband and I made plans with several couples on 147th Drive, (I think there were eleven couples to be exact) to get away for a weekend at Mount Airy Lodge in the Poconos. We had planned this trip for months. Two weeks before we left on the trip, our little son came down with Chicken Pox. A normal childhood disease and I felt it was good to get these contagious diseases over with, especially before he entered Kindergarten. I was sure there would be additional diseases to contend with at a later time. Tony seemed to fare well with the outbreak; the usual itchiness, uncomfortable feeling, the slight temperature and he certainly seemed to be on his way to a full total recovery when we decided, after we received approval from the doctor, to leave for the weekend. We packed the children's clothes and everything else we thought they would need to spend a few days with their Aunt Mary and Uncle Frank, who lived in Whitestone, Queens. Gina and Tony were thrilled because they knew they would have a great time staying with their three cousins, Diana, Frankie and Rosemary.

Since Tony was such a non-bothersome child, Mary and Frank were happy to assist in the baby sitting. Tony may not have been feeling well, but he did not complain. On the second evening at his Aunt Mary's house Tony began spiking a temperature. Mary and Frank immediately took him to their family doctor and Tony was diagnosed with acute appendicitis. Mary relates that he sat very quietly and was very cooperative, even though I am sure he was frightened. Tony was admitted to Astoria General Hospital, the same hospital where he was born. The surgery could not be performed unless we were present, the doctors needed parental consent. We were quickly summoned at the Lodge, and needless to say, without a doubt, we bolted out of there and returned as fast as the trip and the roads would allow. We didn't even go home, we went directly to the hospital. Our signatures were required before they could proceed with the surgery and time was of the essence. Within the hour, Tony was sedated and on his way to the operating room. We waited what seemed to be an eternity, but it wasn't more than one hour that had passed. They wheeled him into the recovery room and barely awake, but enough to render us his great big smile and dozed off into a deep sleep. There was no sleep for us that evening and little did I know then that there would be many other evenings such as this one.

What should have been a simple surgery and a maximum stay of five days (there were no HMO's at that time, with limited hospital stay restrictions) his stay evolved into several weeks. Tony was constantly running a temperature, so he could not be released from the hospital. After completion of a series of tests, the physician concluded that the problem was *not* his appendix, but what had occurred was that one of the chicken pox lesions had manifested itself inwardly, had not erupted on the surface, causing a serious infection in the peritoneal area. After weeks of potent antibiotics, the infection dissipated, the fever disappeared, his general well being was back to normal, and Tony was discharged from the hospital. If for one moment I thought this was my worst nightmare, boy! was I in for many surprises.

My mother used to have a quaint saying "when they are little, you will have little problems, when they are big, you will have big problems", little did I realize, how true some words can be.

CHAPTER TWO

I AM YOUR ANGEL

> *I'll be your cloud up in the sky*
> *I'll be your shoulder when you cry*
> *I'll hear your voice when you call*
> *I am your angel*

Six years ago we adopted a nickname for Tony, it was "Our Angel". This epithet is also inscribed on his tombstone. He received this agnomen due to a physic reading I once had in November 1994, three years before Tony died. On this visit to the physic, he asked to see pictures of my family, and I, without hesitation, proceeded to spread all the wallet photographs I had of my entire family on the table. After viewing all the pictures, the physic, without any forethought sought out the family picture I had of Tony, his wife and his two children and quickly and emphatically stated that Tony was truly "an angel". Of course, I commented that I knew Tony was a good person, very kind and generous, very respectful and I, of course, always viewed him as my angel. The physic repeated again, this time he spoke very forcefully and emphatically avowed in quotation marks that "your son is An Angel". When I questioned the specific meaning of the reading , the physic told me Tony was special, "so very special, a *real* angel". I did not understand the statement at the time, nor did I question the explanation. When I returned home I went directly to Tony's house, I was hesitant to bring the tape home to my own house knowing my husband was, and still is, a skeptic, personified. When I had my son listen to the tape of the session, he just grinned from ear to ear and we all laughed. We continued to laugh every time this tape was mentioned. Tony would stand there, arms akimbo, with the quirkiest smirk on his face and rapidly flapping his arms as wings. My God, my God was someone trying to tell me something back then. Who knows?

Tony was my soul mate from the day of his precious birth. There was a mother-son bond almost instantly from the first outburst of breath, amidst the tears and cries of joy. Of course, little did I know what was in store for the future, both his and mine, and that the tears would someday have a different, dreadful cause. What I did not anticipate was the magnitude of what this bond was to entail, what this bond was to endure, that this bond was going to be clipped and shattered, and what devastation this bond was going to encounter.

Tony was a very pleasant baby and most of all, a well-behaved pleasant little boy. He was sensitive, quiet, sharing and most of all very lovable. He would sit for hours playing with his matchbox cars. He loved to read and at four years of age still taking two-hour naps. He loved to sleep and never gave us a hard time about going to bed at night. At the age of six when he started school he learned to ride his two wheeler, his Schwinn, "green pea picker". Tony's favorite color was always green.

As a toddler, my son had none of the qualities and dynamic traits that his sister possessed. Innately Tony was instilled as a follower, a peacemaker, a friend in need, a confidante, he always had a push-me, pull-me type personality. A child that needed to study, a child that needed to work diligently in order to achieve and ultimately master his goals. Tony, the toddler, also faced challenges but he strove to do his best and did it all very subtly . There were no fanfares, no hooplas, only honest attempts to pave his path and seek his niche in life.

Tony attended St. Pius X Elementary School in Rosedale, New York. First grade was a true test of his learning abilities, his attentiveness, his efforts, and his willingness to learn. It certainly was easier than Kindergarten, due to the fact that in Kindergarten, Tony found it difficult to start out on his own. As I mentioned prior, he was not a leader and so his first venture on his own was challenging and scary for him. Tony proved to be a very good student, immediately liked by friends and teachers. One could see, from the onset, he tried very hard to attain his goals and he did not quit until he achieved what he strove to accomplish.

HOW GREEN WAS HIS VALLEY

His first love was to God, then man,
No greater kindness in this land.
He always gave so willingly,
That's why my "Angel" will always be.

Three years have past on this date.
A most awful day of twisted fate.
We pray to God he is at rest,
To us he was the very best.

T'was green he loved as a child,
His "pea picker" brought a great big smile.
His pulling wagon was never red,
He preferred his green instead.

One of his cars, a perfect dream,
Was surely hued a vivid green.
Napping in that umber shade,
Green grasses, the trees, his favorite glade.

His third love was easy to spy,
Had aspirations towards the sky.
That golf swing he swore was the best,
Was always put to the test.

He had a spark deep inside,
Received a plaque "the longest drive".
The greenest path he loved to play,
Ended too that awful day.

We hope his new home has a scene,
Containing shades of his favorite green.
We know that God now holds his hand,
Guiding Tony through His great green land.

Mom and Dad

Little Blue Angel

And when all hope is gone from there
No matter how far you are from here
It makes no difference who you are
I am your Angel; I am your Angel

Christmas 1968, Tony was almost seven years old, his second grade teacher, Sister Marcella asked him if he would star in her Christmas pageant and have the lead role in "Little Blue Angel" (again a reference to the type of child he was). He graciously accepted, thrilled with the challenge and excited to get his chance to "shine". He rehearsed for weeks, non-prompted, not only his part, but also the parts of the entire cast. He truly was the "star" and succeeded wonderfully. The play was a huge success and Sister Marcella was very impressed, as were the other Sisters at St. Pius convent. Tony was so very young at that time and already had made quite an impression.

Tony went on to play, act, sing in several other shows, some at school, some at home. Again, our boy did "shine". He was truly mom's pride and joy. His dad was equally proud that his son was a dependable, likable, bright little tot, whose comportment was priceless. The shows Tony participated in not only enhanced the major aspect of his talents, but it was the effort, the zeal he exerted into each and every part that became a spectacular achievement. These feats were so important to him because sometimes he needed to prove, especially to his sister, he could do well. Certainly because Gina's challenges were always so well executed. Gina was a perfectionist and so her accomplishments were always a comparison Tony needed to measure up to. This was not something we expected of him, this was something he felt he needed to do on his own. It was very difficult to explain to Tony that their differences were each an individual concept and each precious in their own way. When one excelled in one subject, the other excelled in the opposite direction. Neither one was right nor wrong, just different. His dad and I were always so very proud of both their scholastic abilities and achievements. Neither child gave us cause or concern that their schoolwork would falter or not be up to our expectations.

In reflecting back, my husband and I had a unique childhood, stemming from immigrant parents who spoke very limited English and could not participate in our childhood school activities. My parents especially. They never involved themselves either with the academic part of schooling and certainly not the extra curricula part of education. It was very sad, I remember even to this day, that my parents barely attended my High School Graduation. I am sure they always felt inadequate because of the language barrier and perhaps even embarrassed by their ethnic background. I guess because of my upbringing and my parents' non-participation in schooling, I made it an obsession of mine to involve myself in as much school activity as possible. We, my husband and I, recognized the importance of achieving scholastically and so we were very conscientious to participate in any way we could to have our children succeed. One of our basic rules and the most important one was: "Schooling is of the utmost importance, if you are to make something of yourself. You must do your best. You must follow rules and regulations. You must behave. Never, ever get in trouble at school." We always had this philosophy at home, beginning in Kindergarten and throughout their continued higher education.

There was only one incident in Tony's entire school years that we recall or that was brought to our attention. He was in Kings Park High School, and at that time was an avid follower of the Band Led Zeppelin. Tony took a ball point pen and engraved the word "Led" on a stairwell railing. We received a call from Asst. Principal, (Mrs. Mary LaRosa), regarding Tony's infraction and needless to say we were upset and furious. It wasn't because we would have to pay to have the railing sanded and varnished, but that Tony had disobeyed one of our cardinal rules. Of course, Tony was very apologetic, made amends over and over again, paid the $1.00 to have the banister repaired, but most importantly I think he learned a valuable lesson. Respect for the property of others.

The zeal that Tony put into some of his actions was sometimes his downfall, but he was becoming an outgoing person and needed to make his statement and I guess he needed to make mistakes along the way.

Tony's over-zealousness gradually surfaced in his childhood, then accelerated throughout his teenage years, especially in his acting career. Again, sometimes he just needed to prove to his sister that he could do as well as she did. It was always so obvious that Gina's accomplishments were done to perfection in spite of her impairment. There were times that Tony needed to exceed, and acting was one of those times. Of course, there were times when even rebellion set in, which we anticipated, especially when we forced Tony to participate in all the events that seemed appropriate to us. When we did the rendition of the "Jungle Book", he did not want to be a marching elephant. It might have been that he felt this character role was not his idea of an important part of the play, not a significant part at all. But, due to our coaxing, Tony carried out his participation to the best (or slightly best) of his ability. Except! .

Here is a version of this episode that Maryann Nicholson, my closest friend and Tony's second mom, wishes to elaborate:

"I think it was Tony's sister Gina who had the idea to begin with, she had selected a small group of her friends and formed an ensemble. They put on a skit "Soldier Boy" in her basement. Jean and I picked up on the idea and decided to put on a show the "Jungle Book". Each child had a part in the show. There were lines to learn, songs to sing, costumes to sew, etc. Tony's cousin Dana Evangelista had the starring role of Balou the Bear. Dana also emceed the show as Doctor Doolittle when she "Talked to the Animals". We made such a production of this throughout the summer of 1967, the auditions for the parts, studying lines, creating scenery (even made our own palm trees with oak tag and crepe paper). Everyone, even the parents who lived on the block were getting very enthused about this play. We finally staged the production in Tony's backyard on a quiet warm summer night. It turned out fantastic. All the players were ready, the scenery was in place, and the audience eagerly awaited to see what their own child had accomplished for the past month of rehearsals. Tony and Billy played the part of baby elephants. As the two little elephants were walking around the yard, one of the children in the audience pulled off Billy's elephant tail. Needless to say this upset not only Billy, but Tony as well. Together they tried to beat this kid up. We, of course, interceded and prevented a childhood brawl. No one was the wiser. The show was a big hit, the children were ecstatic that all went well, the parents were really happy to see what their children had accomplished with their spare time during this summer."

-- * --

At an early age one could immediately notice Tony had a fondness for theatrics, especially musicals. Even though he may not have had the lead in each one, he was always willing to share the limelight with all his friends. We never had a problem with Tony sharing his talents, his toys, and/or his possessions. There were exasperating times when Tony shared *too* much. I remember one incident we bought him his much-wanted "Whamo-Airblaster", but no sooner did we return home with it, he let one of his friends play with it and of course, the inevitable, the next day it was broken. I can still hear myself screaming at him for always sharing, giving, and not paying attention to himself or the consequences. You see it was not he who broke the toy, but it was he who was punished.

Was it because Tony thought he needed to give of himself or his belongings in order to receive recognition, to be accepted by his peers, to be their equal or was it simply because it was his nature to be kind and good? I only question this trait now because of the eventual scenario.

If it were not for our memories of all the good times, where would we be? In 1962, the Nicholsons: John, Maryann, Johnny and Billy, moved next door to us and they became very much an important, intricate part of our lives, and they were our closest friends. We became one unit, one close knit family. As a result, our boys who were only eight months apart became brothers to each other. Again, this meshed friendship and bond was to play a part in Tony's future life, but for now let us recall that both Billy and Tony were inseparable.

When we produced our second play "The Time Machine", Tony and Billy were both in third grade and needless to say they needed to be in the same scenes together, the vaudeville skit as *Eddie Cantor* "If you Knew Susie", two of the "Ten Little Indians", cowboys from the "Wild, Wild, West". Tony was disappointed he could not appear with Billy in the "Yellow Rose of Texas", because he did not play the drums at this point of his life. In his teenage years, he developed an obsession with rock music and in trying to emulate Billy's drum talents, Tony learned to play the drums and so he took on another musical accomplishment with which he succeeded.

The following year when they were in fourth grade, Maryann and I produced the play "It's a Small World", Billy and Tony needed to be matadors from Spain together, leprechauns from Ireland, yodelers from Switzerland, sailors from the U.S.A. etc. They were cute, funny, adorable, talented and above all very dedicated to their commitment to participate. (Keep in mind, moms are always prejudiced).

Maybe all this school involvement was not merely for our children's sake, it may very well have been a replacement for something lacking certainly in my childhood, because my childhood had none of the normal participation of family that other families shared. So, as parents, my husband and I were totally dedicated to participate, join, assist, encourage, help with their challenges, whether scholastically or extra curricula activities. We then, together with the Nicholsons, designed and created scenery, sewed the costumes, wrote the score and taught the children to sing, act, dance and, imagine, have fun all at the same time.

Our years in Rosedale were the happiest ever, the best twelve years of our lives. We raised our children as a family. We intermingled with each and every family and became one unit, one support, and one outlet of caring, sharing and enjoying our relationships. The children knew they had an extended loving family with all the families on 147th Drive. The children had so much in common, the same age groups, the same school, and the same interests. They also would get themselves in trouble together.

Gina, who was the leader and mastermind of the group called the "Jet Set" would hold meetings and prepare the agenda for the activities. She ran a very "tight ship" so to speak, she ousted the members who had received demerits because they didn't "tow the line". Billy relates that he and Tony received so many demerits they hardly ever got to sit through one full meeting. At the meetings they would read, sing, play games and make an copious amount of noise. It really didn't matter, they were wholesome, good-natured children with a lot of growing up to do. This is the year 2000 and they still have a friendship they all remember.

Billy also remembers the times that he and Tony not only *did not* listen to Gina, but also *did not* listen to their parents. They were told they were not to leave the confines of 147th Drive without supervision. Did they heed, no way! They were about ten years old and wanted to go fishing. What a fish story they would tell, after they thought they would snag the infamous "big one ". They walked to Woodmere Park, about one mile away, with fishing rods in tow and proceeded to do their thing. They really could not stay too long for they knew they would surely be missed. About one hour later, not one fish on the line, they were walking home, rods over their shoulder, and Tony in the rear. Of course, he wasn't paying attention to where he was going and walked right into Billy's fishing rod and his nose got caught on the hook. But as they related it, the hook impaled itself in Tony's nose. Blood was streaming everywhere. Billy did not panic, he ran home to get help as fast as he could. Tony just sat on the sidewalk and waited for help to arrive. I would love to know what was going on in Tony's mind while he waited for someone to show up. Did he cry? We're not sure, but a neighbor came out of his house, saw this scene, assisted Tony by removing the hook, carefully washed the wound, applied an antibiotic ointment and waited with Tony for us to show up. Did I yell at him? No way. He was hurt and so I was hurt as well. I cuddled him, hugged him and catered to him for the next several days.

There were, as is common in all phases of development, a series of disappointments also. Tony did not excel in sports. Like many dads, who sought to find a Babe Ruth replacement, a Joe Namath act-a-like, a Pele achiever, Tony did not fill his father's expectations in the area of participating sports. That is not to say Tony didn't try hard. He simply was not an athletic child. He seemed very uncoordinated, not agile, not quick, not strong, not above average. He played the fields the best he could, but was never outstanding. He tried his athletic talents, at the urging and coaxing of his father. Tony enrolled in both football and baseball leagues. In little league Tony was second baseman for the 'Orioles' and he certainly was very proud to be a football 'Viking.' Though these juvenile sport years were sometimes trying and exasperating, he later on in life proved to his dad he could do well in sports. He played deck hockey and also joined a bowling league with me and my co-workers, Mr. Al Olingy and Kim, at United States Leasing Corp. We dubbed ourselves the "J-A-K-son 4," an apropos name for **Jean**, **Al**, **Kim** and **son** Tony. In later years Tony was also a team member on the softball league while a novice at Margolin, Winer and Evans. But, Tony's greatest love and greatest achievement of all was golf.

Recollecting Tony's athletic abilities, Andy Daniels, one of Tony's accounting co-workers at M.W. & E. explicitly recounts:

"I met Tony at our firm's softball games and practices. It was during and after the games that I came to know the personality that is uniquely TONY.

There was the extremely competitive, athletic side to Tony that was very obvious. He would play shortstop, the *leader* of the infield. He was the straw that stirred the drink. He wasn't the quickest, strongest or the best player, but his drive was outstanding and his concentration was keen. I would say he was a scrappy determined player."

What Joe and Roberta Bublé, also co-workers, from Margolin, Winer and Evans recall about Tony's sports ability is very touching and memorable, they also recount:

"There are so many wonderful memories we have of Tony. Joe and I met Tony in 1984. At that time, the company was hiring many new people, most of whom were single. We all became good friends and started socializing together. We all enjoyed being a part of the *softball league, valleyball league, and football games.* We also had season Met tickets, we attended parties and spent many Friday Happy Hours together. It was a great time for all of us.

In addition, to the work crowd, there was the separate **deck hockey** crowd. One of our favorite memories of the hockey team was meeting at the Ground Round after the many games. Chicken wings and pitchers of beer were our staple foods. I clearly remember the time when Tony and Joe (my now husband) and some of the other guys had a Tabasco sauce contest. They all had to do shots of hot sauce without drinking any water or beer. A table of college kids next to us tried to copy them and immediately got sick to their stomachs and ran off to the bathroom. Yes, I know it was strange, but that was the gang for you.

-22-

One of the other things we remember about Tony was his competitiveness. Whether it was softball, deck hockey or even board games, Tony always wanted to win at all costs. We remember playing Scattagories, when Tony insisted that "icing the puck" (usually a poor play in hockey), constituted a bad habit. After much arguing, the gang relented and gave Tony his point, but Joe won the game ultimately."

- - * - -

Receiving and reading these excerpts from Tony's co-workers further strengthened my confirmation of his zeal, his enthusiasm, his drive to win, his camaraderie but most of all his friendship, which abounds with us till this day. All the inclusions were heartfelt and sincere. These stories verified my knowledge of Tony's participation in sports, but mostly his warmth in caring and how proud each and every one of his friends were to have known him, even if it was for such a short time.

These Angels of Ours

The Heavenly Herald placed an Ad,
Not to make us cry or make us sad.
God needed Angels to join his crew
Even though it saddened me and you

God called our Angels to His rest,
To join His choirs, He took the best.
To sit beside Him but send us love,
To endear their loved ones from above.

Some Angels steer others to find their way
Some Angels watch the toddlers at play.
Some Angels hear parents as they pray,
Some Angels wipe tears from those who stray.

Our Angels were called from me and you,
Remember, God called His son too.
The special friends of the Almighty One
Who needed Angels to help His Son.

The older Angels help those who ail,
The teenage Angels help those who fail.
The adult Angels help those who cry,
The elder Angels help those who die.

The Baby Angels have a special place,
They live forever in God's holy grace.
The Baby Angel has an eternal smile
Remember this Angel is God's special child.

Let us keep an open heart
Even though we are far apart.
Remember it is for only   a while,
Till again we meet our "Angel" child.

Mom and Dad

-24-

CHAPTER THREE

ME AND MY SHADOW

Just me and my shadow
Strolling down the avenue
Just me and my shadow
Not a soul to tell our troubles to

St. Pius X Elementary School, Rosedale, New York - only one short block from our front door. The friendships acquired both short-term and long-term will never be forgotten. The memories that accompany these friendships will be treasured for a lifetime. Of course, Tony's closest buddy, his best friend, his confidante, his comrade-in-arms, his partner-in-crime, his go-everywhere together chum, his pal of all pals was Billy Nicholson. (Both boys pictured above at age 6)

Billy lived next door, earshot distance, which was great, we never had to fret about them crossing the street; especially since in the summer of 1963 the boy who lived to the right of us did get run over by a car right in front of our house. In respect for anonymity, I shall call the child John. John was playing soldiers with the other neighborhood children when we heard a car screech, and John's mother screaming.

We all ran to the scene of the accident and there we found John with his face pinned under the left front wheel of a Volkswagen driven by one of the tenants on the block. We literally saw John's mother pick up the car with her bare hands and gently remove her son from under the wheel. This reaction of a frantic mother became indelibly embedded on my mind. This was thirty-seven years ago and I can still see the anguish and horror on this mother's face. The excruciating pain on John's face was the mirror image of his mother's horror. Why is this story even remotely relevant to my son's story? Only in the fact that it reflects that a mother suffers the identical pain when a tragedy, such as this, is inflicted on *her* child. We need not question whether it be God sent, man inflicted, self inflicted, it doesn't matter. Childbirth is painful, labor is painful but it pales in comparison to the pain that is experienced when one visually encounters the pain inflicted on their children and the feeling of helplessness becomes immobilizing. Just think of the strength it took for this mother to pick up that car in order to release her son's face.

This family eventually moved from Rosedale to Brooklyn and several years after the accident we met them vacationing at a resort in Pennsylvania. John had many surgeries but seemed to be doing well, as well as could be expected. I personally know there is always residual from a trauma such as theirs and their pain doesn't easily disappear. Afflictions such as these stay with you for a lifetime.

To return to the two peas in a pod, Billy and Tony, who were inseparable, Billy's mom Maryann vividly recalls:

"When I think back, so long ago, to when they (Billy and Tony) were about five years old, my mind goes to one very warm day in the summer when they wanted to have a swimming pool. I knew they always wanted a pool and they talked about one often, but I had no idea that they were going to try to make one all by themselves until one day I heard my mom, Lillian Otto, yelling "the basement is flooded!" That is when we found Billy and Tony had put two hoses, ours and the Varlese's, down the basement steps into my mom's house and turned on the water so they could have a swimming pool.   An indoor one no less. Needless to say they were in **BIG** trouble. Jean and I were picking up water with shovels and soaking it up with large towels, since there were no shop-vacs at that time, for hours on end. Looking back to that day so long ago, it makes us laugh, but at that time, believe me, it just wasn't very funny."

- - * - -

Maryann Nicholson had become the sister I never had. I was an only child and so was she. We were inseparable. We did some weird funny things ourselves so how could we think our sons would be any different.

Together, Maryann and I concocted some crafty projects, but now in retrospect, they were *not* only time consuming but very *unprofitable*. We sat for hours and days on end making bird cages from multi-colored pipe cleaners and a styrofoam base filled with plastic flowers, we adorned the cages with feathery robins, blue jays, canaries, etc. We then drove into neighboring towns, Valley Stream, Rockville Centre, Lynbook and rang doorbells, selling our wares from door to door. Believe me, this was very atypical of our personalities and very out-of-character, but we did it nonetheless. You could say we were young and foolish, very naive, in an ingenuous way.

There was even another time, we, Maryann and I, decided to become especially extra crafty. We both had talents that were dormant for a time and we thought we would again put these hidden talents to some use. Maryann's uncle Hank (her mother's brother) worked in a sweater factory in Maspeth and the cones that housed the wool were being discarded after the wool was used. We took these cones, hand painted them with gold leaf paint, attached them in a circle, side by side, with wooden clothes pins and created a gold wreath to which we would then adhere plastic flowers (again, can you imagine *plastic,* how tacky) but nevertheless they were pretty.   We sold a few on the block to friends and neighbors, and it goes without saying, our families bought many of them. We thought we had a real "gold" (no pun intended) mine going. We felt it was time to expand and sell interstate.

We arose one morning at 4:00 am and headed out to Englishtown, New Jersey. We had heard there was a great flea market there and the clientele purchased anything that was old and used. We figured if we brought our crafts of new items, they would sell like hot cakes.

On our way to Englishtown we got lost, we somehow made a wrong turn and ended up in Trenton, New Jersey, which I think was 75 miles out of our way. We stopped at a diner, asked for directions and headed back. A patron from the diner helped guide us back on track. He rode in the car with us for about twenty- five miles.   You can see this was a long time ago, sometime in 1965 and again, we certainly were very innocent and extremely naive. Could you imagine letting a stranger into your car in the early hours of the morning, across state lines, lost and bewildered in this day and age? (This would never happen today in the year 2000).

Already tired and weary, but very determined, we arrived at our destination, about 9:00am.   We set up our tables, arranged our toted wares and proceeded to sit and sit and sit some more. Of course, buyers would stop at our table, tell us what wonderful, beautiful items we had, but not one would actually purchase anything. We had lunch in the scorching, blaring sun and sat and sat some more. About 2:00 pm a stranger approached our table, lo and behold it was the stranger we had picked up who escorted us to the right exit on the Jersey Turnpike.   He said he just wanted to make sure we made it to our destination. After he left us, Maryann and I looked at each other, laughed our heads off and proceeded to pack up our merchandise at about 3:00 pm and we headed home, disillusioned and disappointed.   Arriving in Rosedale at 6:00 pm, we were too embarrassed and ashamed to bring all our crafts home, without having sold one item. We came up with the brilliant idea to bring them to Maureen Schecker's home. Maureen was Maryann's childhood friend (they recently celebrated their 50th Friendship Anniversary) who lived three miles away from us and so we stored our wreaths in her basement until we felt it was safe to return them home, one at a time. We eventually sold them one by one, again to friends and relatives, but we never let anyone know that our trip to Englishtown, New Jersey was a "total bust", to say the least. The only thing the trip proved was that we too were a little eccentric and adventurous, but we also had the camaraderie that only two really good friends could possibly share. So again, what else should we expect from our sons.

Tony and Billy did get into trouble and did some funny things while they were together, but Tony also did other silly things all by himself. When Tony was six years old he showed a different side of himself. He was being very fickle, a characteristic I had not seen or noticed until this episode. He proved he was a child who already thought about feelings for others, but he was human all the same and amended his feelings accordingly. Here is one example:

It was sometime in 1968, Gina and my husband wanted a pet. We had just lost our cat Bimbo, which Gina had adopted from a neighbor several years prior, but this time Gina and her dad wanted a dog. I was never, and still am not, keen on pets, because they need attention and care. The children always made statements such as, "I'll take care of it, I'll feed it, I'll train it, I'll walk the dog" etc., but after the first couple of weeks, the novelty of having a pet wears off and then who was left with the chores of maintaining a pet, ME. Even though I had a slight aversion towards pets, I was always a pushover when it came to trying to please my children. My first reaction was to make a statement to both Gina and her dad, "If you decide to get a dog, I will leave home", hoping this would deter them from the anticipation of buying a dog. One day we proceeded to visit the local pet shop and there just happened to be the most adorable, cuddly

West Highland White Terrier. Before we entered the shop, Tony Jr. looked at me and said "if you run away from home mommy, I will come with you."

Gina and her dad were ecstatic about this little white ball of fuzz and then I saw the look on Tony's face. He really didn't know how to break the news to me that he no longer agreed with me about running away from home. He quietly remarked, "Mommy, I think you'll have to run away by yourself, I'm staying with daddy." He, like his father and his sister, fell in love with this puppy, which we eventually purchased, brought home and christened "Westie". Not a very original name, but it fit him perfectly and so it stayed. The dog's proper AKA (American Kennel Association) name was Romulus Cennen. This name was so uppity and so very proper and certainly difficult to say, that "Westie" himself responded promptly to his new name.

Billy and Tony still had a relationship that matched no other, what one wanted to do, the other would follow. Mix and match, they were Frick and Frack and we loved them to no end. There were so many episodes where they proved to be so inseparable.

Maryann recalls yet even another episode , maybe not so funny at the time, but a very noteworthy recollection:

"We bought some land upstate New York when my son Johnny was about ten, Billy was eight and my daughter Nancy was an infant. We had a mobile home on this tract of land and we spent our summers and some of our winter vacations there. It was a great place for the kids to grow up. My two sons loved it and Tony loved it just as much, if not more! They made friends with Bruce; the farmer that lived next door and they did everything with Bruce, and for Bruce. They helped him with the haying, the planting, milking the cows and even shovel manure out of the barn. (They never cleaned their own rooms, but they helped clean the barn with the terrible odor. I could never understand that!).

We would make the trip upstate almost every weekend and then for a few weeks in the summer and winter also. Every Friday afternoon Tony would sit on the steps to our house just waiting for us to ask him if he wanted to go away for the weekend. When we did, he would figuratively fly home to ask his parents if it was okay with them that he join us. We would pack up the car and start the three hour trip to Halcottsville, New York. We would always stop at Kingston, New York and have lunch or dinner depending on the time of day. The diner was always our first stop. When we finally reached our mobile home, the boys would always jump out of the car first. They were always so happy we arrived after what seemed to be a very long trip.

One Friday, in particular, Tony's parents had made plans to visit relatives, and so he was told he couldn't come with us. This visit had to be special to deny Tony permission to come with us because his parents knew how much he loved to be with us (especially with Billy). We felt so bad that Tony couldn't come with us but we packed up the car and we left for upstate without him.

As I said, it was a long drive and usually we would play word games to help pass the time more quickly. On this trip my sons were seated in the back seat and they were unusually quiet. I knew they felt bad about Tony not being there with them. We had the radio on but no one said much of anything. We arrived in Kingston two hours later and stopped at our usual diner. The boys got out of the back seat and then much to our surprise, guess who else got out of the car...Tony! All three of them were laughing and laughing! He had hidden on the floor, and my sons covered him with blankets so we wouldn't see him and we drove two hours with him in the car not knowing it. (Author's note: We knew Tony was playing at another neighbor's home and so for two hours Tony was not missed. When the Nicholsons arrived in Kingston, they telephoned to notify us that he was there and well.)

After arriving at the upstate home and the boys went to bed and after we spoke to the Varleses, my husband and I reflected on the two-hour trip and only then did we realize why the boys had been so quiet.

Every time Tony came upstate with us the first thing he would say when he got out of the car was 'This is Paradise!'. We now find happiness in knowing that we gave Tony those wonderful weekends that he loved so much, where they could all run, play, laugh and feel so much freedom away from the city streets."

- - * - -

One of my own recollections is of a weekend we also spent with the Nicholsons, Gina and Tony Jr. included, is as follows:

I recall hiking in the woods and also enjoying the great outdoors. No wonder my son was always so anxious to make the trip with them. Being out of the city and into nature is the most serene feeling a person can experience. The smell of the freshly sprouting buds on the pine trees, the visual greenery that was no soothing to the eye, relaxing and calm. There was no noise from traffic, no whistles blowing from the railroad crossing, no roaring of the low flying planes over Brookville Blvd., ready to set down on Runway 7 of John F. Kennedy Airport. Just silence and peacefulness.

On this one particular Sunday, we were having a barbecue before we were going to head back home. The Nicholson's neighbor Bruce brought over some wild leeks that had been growing in his garden. The guys started the charcoal fire and Maryann and I made the salad, of course, we included the leeks Bruce gave us, all of them. We certainly did not want to discard any so we overloaded the salad with the leeks. Hamburgers and hot dogs were placed on the grill, corn on the cob was boiling in the pot, the salad was seasoned and we sat down to consume whatever was there so we did not have to carry leftovers back home.

After eating as much as we could stuff ourselves with , Maryann and I started to clean up. Johnny, Maryann's oldest son, and

Tony Jr. came into the cabin to tell us there were still two hot dogs on the grill we did not use. Trying to salvage everything, we admonished the boys to go back outside and finish grilling the remaining hot dogs. I instructed my son Tony to make sure mine was charred. I preferred to have my hot dogs very very well done. About five minutes later Johnny and Tony returned into the kitchen with the "burnt" hot dogs. John Sr. and I each took one and managed to finish off the salad with all the leeks and a lot of Italian bread.

We packed up, left for Rosedale, arrived about 8:00 pm and got the children ready for bed. About eleven o'clock in the evening I developed severe abdominal cramps. I doubled over in pain. I got very sick to my stomach and became very diaphoretic. I immediately drank some Pepto-Bismol and it settled the cramps temporarily. At about two o'clock in the morning, I awoke trembling uncontrollably, my nerves were spasmodic and I could not stand up. The first thought that ran through my mind was that "the homegrown leeks were poisonous". It was so late I wouldn't dare call Maryann or John to see if they were feeling okay. John and I had been the ones to clean the salad bowl of all the leeks and John had most of them, so I surmised, if I was this ill, I can't imagine how sick John must be. My husband finally gave me several glasses of warm milk, managed to get me to lie down and the tremors ceased.

The following morning, I immediately called Maryann to see how John was doing. Her response was that "John went to work, he's fine. He wasn't sick at all and neither was anyone else in her family".

At dinner that evening, my husband and I were discussing my symptoms and the fact that no one else was ill was a surprising factor. I think Tony was about ten years old at that time and he quietly, innocently and seriously remarked, "I wonder if the charcoal lighter fluid that I poured on your hot dog to get it charred had anything to do with you getting sick, Mom?". Lo and behold, the answer to the dilemma, the charcoal fluid is petroleum based and because it was burnt into the hot dog and with all the relish on the hot dog you could not taste it, but it was soaked into the hot dog enough to have left a residue which I had ingested. It was a mild case of petroleum poisoning which attacked my nervous system and caused the tremors. This episode became a laughing matter only after I proved that I was okay and none- the- worse for having ingested this fluid. It was Tony's absolute sincerity, his naiveté, his innocence of knowledge, which made this escapade a comical memorable recollection.

The bond of friendship that we and the Nicholsons shared then and the bond we share now can never be described in common language. It is a deep feeling of respect, honor, but most of all love for one another. I know deeply that our loss is also their loss. We do share our memories and acknowledge their grief at the loss of one of their other sons.

Maryann and I had so much in common, both being only children, we bonded more than friends usually do. We did many things together, one year we joined ceramic classes. I was not as finite and detailed as Maryann was, but I managed to create some very beautiful pieces. What still is vivid in my mind even today is the exquisite Nativity Scene Maryann created, and I remember being very envious. We did flower arranging at J.J. Newberrys, we tried to lose weight by joining Lucille Roberts. I am not sure we had to lose ten pounds between us, but we joined anyway. But of all our trials and experiments, our innate love and talent was certainly music. We loved music the most, I loved to sing and play the accordion and Maryann was a professional dancer and eventually became a dance teacher. (As of this writing she still teaches dancing). With these joint talents, we decided to teach the neighborhood children to sing and dance. Not only would we be doing something we loved, but we would also keep the children involved in a wholesome project for the summer and also give them something constructive to do. I have already recounted the production of the "Jungle Book" in our backyard in Chapter Two, but **Maryann wishes to add:**

"Because of the "Jungle Book" being such a success in the backyard, and at the same time Jean and I had become very good friends with Tony and Billy's first grade teacher, Sr. Carmel Marie. When she found out about the success of the show, she suggested we put the show on in the auditorium of the school and even charge admission, 25 cents for children and 50 cents for adults. In addition to giving the rest of the neighborhood a chance to see our accomplishments, we made money for the school. Again, this show proved successful, theatrically and financially. Sr. Carmel Marie had us putting on shows with other students in the school after that. We did everything and anything to help out. We taught the students dance routines, sang songs and we would stay up late at night (sometimes till 2:00 am) making costumes out of any kind of material we could get our hands on, even plastic tablecloths. (Jean does remember the green plastic tablecloths with the big white flowers). We made the cutest short skirts out of them! Jean's husband Tony Sr. ran off the programs at work to save the school money. My husband John and Tony Sr. also constructed a large stage for the school. We managed to get other neighbors involved to help us with the scenery so that these productions would be as professional as could be and wouldn't cost the school any money.

Again, since Tony and Billy were always glued together, what would be more appropriate than teaching them the song and dance **Me and My Shadow.** They sang and did an easy little soft shoe tap dance, messed up a lot and laughed a lot too. They were just the best and had to be the cutest. I can't remember if this was the first or second grade, but growing up they were always *me and my shadow*.......in fact, at Tony's wedding reception, Billy was his best man, they again approached the microphone and sang the song **Me and My Shadow,** they flubbed the dance steps a little, but who cared, they were buddies. This memory I shall never forget."

MY YOUNG CHILD

You were the light that helped brighten our days.
You fulfilled our expectations in many ways.
As an infant you were as good as gold.
As a child you were easy to hold.
As a teenager you gave us sleepless nights,
Yet as an adult you did all that was right.

No parent could have felt so proud.
You always stood out in a crowd.
Your humor, your loving caring ways,
Received from friends nothing but praise.
Our days are now dark without you here.
Our nights are filled with dread and fear.

Your pain has transferred to us all,
But with God's help we will endure this fall.
At times you might have been hard to bear,
But a love like yours was indeed so rare.
Your life ended so forgiving,
But hard for us to go on living.

A loving memory you'll always be,
To your sister, friends and family.
Especially for Mom and Dad,
A beautiful son is what we had.
You will always be a treasure to hold.
We pray your sons will fill your mold.

Mom and Dad

CHAPTER FOUR

I DID IT MY WAY

Regrets I had a few
But yet again too few to mention
I did what I had to do
And then I grew without exemption

In 1973 we moved from Rosedale to Kings Park, simply because the house was getting small for us and we felt the need to expand. We were seeking better schools for the children and room for them to spread their wings, so to speak, and reach out to new adventures, new beginnings, yet never forgetting what we were leaving behind. We knew we could never replace what we had already gained in friendship, loyalty and love from our Rosedale group, but the move was something we felt we needed to do, if we were to ever forge ahead. There are so many other stories about the Rosedale group I would love to relate. The backyard parties, the block parties, the Halloween parties, the New Year's Eve parties, the 'if you buy a television' the block needed to celebrate and have a party. Maybe it was the age we were at the time, but we did have our share of parties and fun.

Our children were no different, they shared the good times with us and good times amongst themselves. Of course, there were rough times when there were also silly disputes among themselves. There were playful accidents, one in particular I recall, when the boys were playing at a construction site. There was a home being built on the next block and the boys, the Senas, the Nicholsons, the D'Angelos, 'Bange' Evangelista and Tony included, decided to help with the construction. All was going well until one of the boys heaved a piece of a 2 x 4 block of wood over the roof, and where do you think it landed on the other side of the roof? Right on Tony's head. Here we go again, the piece of wood landed point down and gashed a hole in the frontal portion of Tony's head. We were able to stop the bleeding, applied some butterfly stitches, bandaged the wound and I hugged the daylights out of him. I wouldn't dare scream out loud, but it hurt me just as much as it hurt him.

The time Tony and Billy were playing firemen, climbing up the wrought iron trellis on the Nicholson's front porch. Only this time, it was Billy who slipped, fell on the concrete stoop and cracked his two front teeth. I really felt bad, because I too considered Billy my other son.

Gina also, together with the older group of children, had many scrapes herself. The one I need to mention, due to a kindness of one of the Rizzo boys, was when Gina was riding her two wheeler up and down the street, she was about eleven years old at the time, she was rounding one of the corners that had a patch of sand and so the bike skidded and she went straight into the oncoming traffic. A car was driving by and had to apply the brakes quickly to avoid hitting her, so the screech was heard clear to our house in the middle of the block. Of course, I started running towards the screech and there I see Mario Rizzo carrying Gina in his arms heading towards us. I immediately thought she was hit by the car so I began screaming, the neighbors came running, we all huddled around Mario and Gina. Gina needed medical attention immediately since she had road burn from skidding on the asphalt pavement and the sand had been deeply imbedded in her knee. It was a long healing process and she was house bound for a couple of weeks. Mario Rizzo, was a few years older than Gina, yet he still showed his concern. He called several times and visited to see how she was progressing. Mario Rizzo has gone to heaven seventeen years ago, but he will always be remembered by the Varlese family for his kindness, caring and genuine concern for our daughter. God certainly does reach out and call home the very best. Mario, we still think of you and you will always be in our prayers.

The good times, the great times, including the sad times come with us wherever we go. Forty miles of separation does not change the people, the memories and the love we all shared.

At the time we moved, Gina was a teenager and Tony was almost thirteen. We agonized over what we thought this change of location might do to both of them. These were crucial years, removing them from their "families" and friends was not going to be an easy task. Gina, with her impediment, had to meet new classmates who were not cognizant of her physical impairment and what reaction they would have when it surfaced. Again, another gauntlet around her neck. We also had trepidation about Tony having to meet another challenge, another major hurdle in making new friends. Tony, at this time of his life, was still very shy when he encountered someone for the first time. He warmed up slowly, but once he felt comfortable with the associations there was never a question of his loyalty and friendship. He was always steadfast in his allegiance and his word was as solid as "Gibraltar".

Gina attended Kings Park High School, Tony was enrolled at Fort Salonga Elementary School for one year, then on to Rogers Middle School. Their cohesiveness with the new classmates went very smoothly. We were elated that the transition went better than we expected. Gina melded in immediately and was overwhelmed at the new reception of friendliness. Tony did have a sense of loss of familiar surroundings, but after a short while he adjusted. We did notice he kept his friends to a minimum. Again, he was not as out-going as his sister. His confidence still had to be nurtured. He was just the average boy on the block.

In trying to capture some of the Rosedale experiences, Tony did enroll in the drama class and was again happy to be selected as one of the star actors in the rendition of the *The Lions Den*. He became very articulate, started to come out of his thin surface shell, and got excellent grades in all his subjects and this proved to be the catalyst for starting his new found personality. He became a little more daring. In fact, one day, at the age of fourteen, I received a call from one of our new neighbors; she notified me that Tony was seen driving around the neighborhood in *MY* car. He had no license, never took a driving lesson, but he was so sure of himself that he felt he could master anything on his own and he felt so invincible. This venture was probably done on a dare by one of his friends and Tony needed to prove he was just 'great'. But, this was only the beginning of what was to be a reversal teenager; he started to try his luck at being rebellious.

We had on-going arguments over his long unruly hair, his selection of heavy metal music, his faded cut-off ripped blue jeans, his "I can master anything" attitude. Where was the shy boy I once had, where did all this confidence emanate from? I am not sure, certainly peer pressure might have had something to do with Tony's new change of personality. "You are the company you keep", a statement I once heard that proved too true at that time. Of course, there were the everyday battles of right from wrong, taking a fad a tad too far, fitting in with the crowd, in short, trying to get away with 'the sowing of his wild oats'. These teenage years were very trying to me. My husband, being a man, had a different viewpoint of what a teenager should or should not get away with. There were curfews Tony found difficult to cope with, the dinner time rule (must be at the table by 5:30 pm, every day, no exceptions). My contention about the dinner time rule was that this was the time for adult conversation, finding out what is happening at school, at work, at home and listening to everyone's outside constraints. We discussed timely current problems, future explorations, but most of all I felt there would always be a connection that had family values, which I firmly believed in and tried to adhere to.

My own upbringing was very disjointed, simply because I had parents who spoke very little English and had many cultural differences and ethnic ideologies that made it difficult or simply impossible to have my idea of an 'Ozzie and Harriet' type family. I always envisioned, when I was growing up, having a family so close knit with a bond no one could ever break, no problem that could not be tackled, no solution that could not be found, no mistake that could not be rectified. In general, a communicating family that could express their thoughts, ideas, aspirations and above all whatever dilemma they might dwell upon either at the present time of something perceived for the future. I learned early in my childhood and then somewhat later in life, the fact that if you pray you need not worry, only worry if you don't pray. How I wish this was really true in what was to be a parent's worst nightmare, certainly mine.

I guess, like many other parents, when you have a teenager, there is never a true full night's deep sleep. Tony was a typical teenager, trying to spread his wings, trying to stretch his curfews, trying to test my endurance, trying to live life to the fullest and yet trying to stay within the restricted confines of house rules.

As a normal teenager, Tony was no different than his peers. He had his rebellious stage, his statement "this is another generation, Mom". He was always trying to fit in; I always felt he wanted to measure up to his other friends. He had his trials with the *long hair, the loud heavy metal music, missing curfews, sassy remarks etc*. There certainly were times when I felt lost and I wasn't reaching him. He started to develop this 'Who Cares' attitude. What I see now was a teenager whose outward demeanor was playing out a somewhat defiant young boy who needed to emulate his friends, and would rather play the trying game with us instead of disappointing his friends.

Sad to say, depending on your point of view, I set very stringent rules. I imposed curfews. I scrutinized their friends; I tried to evaluate them, either male or female, yet I *accepted* all their friends into our home openly and respectfully. I was very caring and welcomed their presence, because of my limited childhood experiences; I needed to make sure my children would not lack this very essential element of childhood, adolescence and certainly their adulthood, a host of many friends.

This chapter wouldn't be long enough for me to include all of Tony's friends, near, distant, classmates from grammar school, from high school, college, colleagues at work, new neighbors he met after he got married, employers who became his friends, clients who considered themselves his friends, his Rosedale buddies, his Kings Park pals, the list goes on and on.

After we moved to Kings Park, Tony did enlarge his circle of friends, yet continued to keep in touch with the Rosedale crowd and tried to shuffle his time to incorporate both groups. Were his Kings Park friends the same as the Rosedale group? I don't think so. The Rosedale bunch were like family, they always looked after one another. This new group of friends had yet to be tried. I remember one incident that still makes me tingle.

One afternoon I returned home from work and upon opening up the front door, I got the biggest whiff of peppermint. It seemed the house had been over-run with peppermint trees or possibly eucalyptus. I searched, I scouted, then I finally questioned my son. Since Tony found it very difficult to lie to us, he confessed to the fact that he and Warren, had conjured up this fantastic idea to create a mural on my kitchen wall. They didn't use paint or crayons, they used Colgate toothpaste. After using several tubes of toothpaste, they needed to wash it off before I got home. They then proceeded to use Pine- Sol.

The odor from the combination of peppermint toothpaste and outdoor pine permeated our home for weeks. It wasn't a bit funny at that time, but this was the least troublesome of episodes that I can remember.

The escapade of more significance was when Tony borrowed his dad's tools from the garage (never to return again, I might add). It seems he and his friends wished to construct a wooden fort in one of the secluded treed areas on the grounds of the Kings Park Psychiatric Center. It wasn't so much the loss of the tools, or the shack that they had built, but the fact that one day Tony's dad went looking for him (and the tools) and found them all comfortably seated in a circle in the shack, laughing their heads off. The glassy look in their eyes, the unusual smell of weird smoke gave credence immediately that they were experimenting with "Pot", or better known as marijuana.

Upon the sight of his father arriving, Tony sank sheepishly, scared out of his wits, and slithered out of the shack and ran home as fast as he could. He knew he was in for a BIG lecture and, of course, the punishment and grounding that would ensue. I recall four weeks of grounding was bestowed upon him. The saddest part was not the punishment or the grounding, but the fact that Tony knew he had disappointed his father, had deeply hurt him by not abiding by the rules. If Tony ever tried to experiment again, after that, it certainly was kept a good secret, for we never had any suspicion of his smoking since.

Some of Tony's closest teenage friends in Kings Park were Angela, Emile, Warren, Kopeck, Eddie, and Andy to mention a few. There were also his acquaintances at school, all of whom Tony respected and shared his days with, but most of his afternoons were usually spent with the friends who lived in the development, the ones within the Charter Oaks boundary and those especially on Twin Oaks Drive.

As in Rosedale, there were Kings Park escapades that were real upsetting also. A hard one to forget was the episode when

Tony's sister Gina had saved some money from her meager salary working at the Kings Park Psychiatric Center after school as an aide apprentice (washing dishes, mopping floors, etc). I recall the amount to be $11.00. Gina had carefully, or so she thought, hid the money somewhere in our dining room breakfront. Gina still swears it was hidden very safely. Several days later the money had mysteriously disappeared. We searched the house high and low, to no avail; the money could not be found anywhere. Finally, we placed the blame on Tony or even perhaps one of his friends, since his friends always had freedom in our home (I guess it was my fault for being so open and trustworthy with visitors, probably because I knew my children would never take anything that didn't belong to them, and I just surmised neither would anyone else who visited our home). In either case, be it Tony or his friends, he was blamed and he who received the wrath of Gina and myself. We punished him, we grounded him and then one day we returned home to find Tony was missing (he supposedly ran away from home). I screamed and cried and then the scene became almost comical when I discovered Tony had left his glasses behind. How far could he venture with his poor eyesight?

We combed the neighborhood for a few hours and finally his dad found him hiding in that make-shift hut the boys had built on the hospital grounds, three blocks away from home. He seemed happier than we were that he was found. The entire escapade was a total of three hours, as I recall, but it felt like days to me, not knowing, always fearing the worst. Even after we laughed about him leaving his glasses home, I was still quite upset. When he entered the door with his dad he still maintained his innocence about the missing money. At this point the money seemed so trivial. He was home and that was all that mattered. I was so elated to see him back home, I kind of lost track of why he had left in the first place, but I don't think Gina ever forgot the incident. She always worked so hard to save her earnings, which she did effectively. Tony on the other hand was, even then, the more splurging one. Whatever he saved, he knew how to spend it. Tony really loved to save but loved to spend it on something unique, different, something he could share with others, make others happy, something that would certainly leave an impression. He was not then or even later in life ever selfish.

Even at an early age Tony demonstrated a virtue of giving. He saved a tidy sum of money from his earnings as a part-time clerk at Pathmark and gave it to us for our 25th Wedding Anniversary. In 1981, he gifted us with twenty-five $50.00 bills, a total of $1,250 which paid for our trip to Bermuda to re-capture our honeymoon of 1956. Besides this being an enormous amount of money for one so young, it was his exuberance of giving that made it all the more precious. He always felt it was in giving that he would show his love. His giving came from his heart, which was truly Tony. His love came from his soul, which was truly my son.

Getting older, but still not wiser. There were nights when Tony managed to convince me he *really* needed to follow the band Zebra, for he was their 'roadie' and just *had* to be there. Rock music and I did not gel whatsoever. Tony had a lot of convincing to do in order for me to approve his ventures. After he told me over and over again that "I was a very antiquated person", I would sometimes submit to the pressures brought upon me by him *and his dad*, but rest assured I would not fall asleep until his Firenza pulled into our driveway. Every passing light coming down Twin Oaks Drive cast its beam into our bedroom and only when the squealing sound of his tires turning into our driveway was it a welcome relief. The front door would slowly and quietly open and close, Tony thought if he did not make noise I would be none the wiser as to the exact time he sauntered in. Then the following morning, after a few rounds of arguing about the time he came in, whether it would be early, on time, or late, his remarks would always be the same, "Mom, I am a very responsible person and I would not do anything stupid". My retort to that statement would be, "It is not you I think would do anything wrong, it is the other guy, I worry about". I felt only the weirdos go out *late* at night, there are drunk drivers, tired drivers, reckless drivers on the road late at night and they may cause the accident. Tony's comeback would be "there is a time for every season under heaven, a time to play, a time to cry, a time to live and a time to die, (these words he had learned from a song in one of his plays). When it is my turn mom, you can cry then. Only God knows what is in store for me and you losing sleep is not going to help or change it". Was Tony philosophizing or being a prophet of some sort at this time of his life?

All this worrying, all those sleepless nights and then what? Death. Any death, but especially suicide, promotes the questions. Why? How did this happen? Where was I when the desolation took hold? When did I become so blind I did not see the deep despair? Were there calls of help I did not hear? There are no answers, only more questions and again the whys, how come, where, when and then most of all the *'what ifs'*.

When I was in therapy, the same questions were asked over and over again, time after time. Sometimes one becomes so desperate and frustrated and logic proclaims that the questions should not be asked in the first place, but since when does grief present with logic.

In my heart of hearts, I know that if Tony could have had a glimpse into the future, and was able to see the devastation his passing brought upon the entire family, relatives, employers and friends, he would not have pursued his demise. As defiant as he may have been at times, he was always a caring, loving person. He would not knowingly hurt, not even slightly, the family he loved so much. It was not in his nature to be non-caring, certainly not selfish, as so many victims of suicide are perceived to be. *If only* I could have lifted his pain. *If only* I could have spared him the grief of what he perceived to be a loss. *If only* I could have taken his place. *If only* I could have protected him. The *if onlys* could go on forever. The whirlpool of *if only* just eddies deeper and deeper into that black hole of unanswered whys.

IF ONLY

If only I could at least dream
Maybe I would see,
My son's bright smiling face
Looking down on me.

If only I could feel
The presence of his touch,
Maybe then the pain I have
Wouldn't hurt quite so much.

If only I could hear,
The sound of his laughing voice,
Maybe hear him whisper,
Mom, "I had no other choice".

If only I could sense,
The sweetness he always had,
Maybe then the loneliness I have,
Wouldn't feel quite so bad.

Is Tony really happy?
If only I really knew,
I know he's in the arms of God,
My instincts say it's true.
Mom & Dad

Could I say he was perfect? Far from it. His teenage years left much to be desired. He sometimes would rebel directly at me at the issuance of my strict guidance. He would defy the times I imposed his curfews. He would sass back at me for my rendition of what his mode of dress should be. Where or where did the long hair style ever resurrect itself? I felt it should have been left behind with the Indians and the Colonial Wig Party. I dare not mention the numerous times we bantered back and forth over this particular controversy. Tony had thick dark shoulder length hair that could and did sometimes resemble a girl. Some of our elderly relatives, with failing eyesight, remarked at times and questioned who this girl was, when confronting Tony.

Of course he would state, "I am a man", so "Who cares?" These were the years of constant remarks, such as "So What", "I know what I'm doing", "Mom, let me be, let me grow up". His famous statement "Can I not make my own mistakes and then am able to correct them?" to which I would always have a comeback, in retrospect how ironic; "some mistakes may be too hard to correct, if they can be corrected at all". Yet, Tony needed to sow his oats, as all young men would find as a necessity and an essential part of growing up. His one other statement stands clear in my mind at this junction of his life was, "the bond that joins us is the bond that will separate us". He knew full well that my chastising was for his own good, not my own. Deep down, in his wisdom, he knew that I nagged him to do the right things, he knew we wanted him to be the man we could and would be proud of.

"Mom, sometimes I know I screw up", this he would tell me when I became angry with him for not conforming to my standards. He would then add "remember I will always amend my errors". His death is the one screw up that could and never will be amended. So how could you expect me to go on, without my only son? The haunting, the flashbacks, the philosophical comments, repeat and repeat in my mind, day in and day out, a horrendous torture.

CHAPTER FIVE

STAIRWAY TO HEAVEN

There's a lady who's sure
All that glitters is gold
And she's buying a stairway to heaven

The usual good times during Tony's teenage years were experienced in due course of events. I could look back and see how handsomely dressed he was in a sharp light gray cut-a-way tuxedo to attend his junior prom. At that time his hairdo was of the utmost importance, the crucial element of his appearance and of his ultimate concern. Tony commandeered his sister, maybe even bribed her a little, to be the stylist for this momentous occasion. Was he dapper? Why, of course. (but then I was always a bit prejudice when it came to my children). Above all else, he had that certain glimmer of sheepishness, that reassured demeanor of confidence, the debonair suave gleam, the "I could do no wrong, I am the best" image of himself. Self-proclaimed I'm sure. He escorted Laura, one of his classmates, who wore a beautiful deep bright pink silk and lace bodice gown and , of course, Tony made absolutely sure the corsage he purchased was appropriate and certainly color coordinated. This was in 1980, it seems like an eternity has passed since that joyous night.

During his junior and senior years at Kings Park High School, Tony was fortunate in obtaining a part-time stock clerk position at Pathmark Supermarket in Commack. Everything he tackled he worked at diligently and achieved the best he could accomplish, even a tedious position such as stock clerk was always so well executed. Tony took this job, even though humble, very seriously, he never missed a day of work, proved to be very conscientious and a loyal good worker. In fact, one day I received a telephone call from the store manager who asked to speak to Mr. Varlese Sr. personally. I thought Tony may have gotten himself into some kind of trouble, but the opposite was true. The manager was inquiring about whether we had more sons like Tony still at home, for he seldom found employees who would work so diligently for a mere minimum wage. This only confirmed what we already knew about Tony's good qualities. We were very proud that his manager took the time to inform us about Tony's work ethics and diligence.

College Years

You know you have a happy son, that when college selection was forthcoming, he calmly, with a positive attitude, stated that he did not wish to go away to college. He preferred to select a local college where he could be near his family. He chose C.W. Post, L.I. University, enrolled in a four-year accounting course. He knew from early on in his teenage years he wanted to be a Certified Public Accountant. He was happy to commute the forty-five minutes on good days. He was self confident, self-assuring, so very positive in his choice and so he excelled scholastically. He maintained a 3.75 average.

Tony never seemed to come home with a problem; at least not one he felt he could not solve on his own. Because we were always very supportive of all his and Gina's endeavors, Tony developed the necessary positive learning attitude any parent would be proud to boast about.

Tony had his career path mapped out very early in life. He did well in all his subjects, but mathematics was always his favorite. This was a subject he could grasp immediately, and sharply, one that would use all his potential to the fullest. The subject he was the least interested in was science, but that was acceptable. We didn't expect him to like or excel in every subject. We were thrilled he knew what he liked and that he pursued his own path. On the other hand, Gina excelled in the science field and so we felt there was an even compromise, an even balance in the scope of possible avenues they would embark upon.

Even though Tony did well in those four years of college, there were always his personal trials to contend with. He did not lack for friends and so this is where we, him and I, had our confrontations. You should keep in mind that I was an *only* child, raised in a very old-fashioned cultural household, reared in my first eleven years by an Italian immigrant paternal grandmother. I was taught the basics, home economics, cooking, cleaning, knitting etc. and we also did a lot of praying. There was no socializing with classmates or friends. We did not have a television, or a radio. This may sound like one of those stories "I walked five miles to get to school", but I need to reinforce my limited childhood in order to explain why and how I tried to raise my children. My methods were not from a textbook; I only had the innate family upbringing from a Walton Mountain atmosphere. I was educated, to a degree, subjected to Roman Catholic teachings only, which as of this writing did prove to be my salvation. What I lacked in upbringing was the more liberal ideology of modern civilization. This is not an excuse, just a clarification as to why I felt I had the need to scrutinize and monitor my own children's whereabouts. It wasn't that I was inquisitive, my need was that of concern and safety, above all less, for both my children. This is where Tony and I would have head-to-head confrontations. He tried to understand my upbringing but found it very difficult to abide by my ideas of what a young boy should or should not do. I had the same arguments with my mother; for she still found a need to reprimand me when she thought I was being too lenient with my children. So, I lost both times.

While working at Pathmark and attending college classes, Tony established new friendships. His closest friend John Nicolette was both a classmate and a co-worker at Pathmark. They formed a tight bond at that time that endured for years. This bond was severed by the death of my son. Tony also became a friend with Tod Skidmore and his fiancé Jean. There also was a young girl whom he cared for immensely and their friendship lasted a very long time. After fifteen years of separation this beautiful girl attended Tony's wake and only then I mentioned to her *how much* he had cared for her.

Before Tod had become engaged to Jean, he spent many weekends with us. He, unlike some of Tony's earlier friends, was a very quiet young man, very serious minded and also very conscientious, so Tod and Tony were sure to get along famously. In fact, Tony was Godfather to Tod and Jean's first born, Michele. I remember, Tony was so proud to be honored with such an undertaking and gave this precious child a memorable gift, a beautiful gold cross, apropos for a Christening.

In the winter of 1978, Tod and Jean, Gina and her husband Bob, John Nicolette and of course, my son decided to go away for a weekend skiing at Hunter Mountain in the Catskills. Was I afraid to agree to the trip? You bet your life. I visualized Tony heading down the tallest slope and cascading into a mound of snow, avalanching towards a mogul and breaking some of his bones. Here again, for some reason I always feared the worse. Tony was very accident prone and very daring, fearless and sometimes did *stupid* things, so it would be inevitable that Murphy's Law would prevail. It so happens on this particular trip there were no major catastrophes, just some simple frost bites, the usual places like his fingertips and toes, but the most evident place was the tip of Tony's nose, which was red as Rudolph's and as icy as a vanilla frosted milkshake.

Tony eventually did become an avid skier and only from what he related, he thought he was pretty good. The verdict was not in and I refused to share his enthusiasm. Oh! the pulls, the tugs continued to occur during these teenage years of growing up. I mentioned Tony was accident prone, if you're keeping score here is Tony's second trip to the emergency room at St. John's Episcopal Hospital in Smithtown. One evening, I recall, receiving a telephone call from Tod. Tony and Tod were in the emergency room at the hospital. It seems that Tony was over zealous at his work and was trying to speed up the unpacking of boxes in order to stock the shelves, *fast and furious*. He was using a sharp one-sided blade cutter and swung it towards his body instead of away from it, and managed to slit his left arm from the wrist up towards his elbow. He, luckily, did not sever an artery, but the amount of blood loss was enough to frighten all his fellow workers. It even became a bit humorous, Tod recalls, no one could speedily find sufficient bandages at the time, but then quickly someone had the foresight to open a package of sanitary napkins and wrap Tony's wrist until they arrived at the hospital. This trip to the emergency room required fifteen stitches.

What I remember is that when I got off the phone with Tod, my visualization took effect again, the frightening thought that Tony would bleed to death, my legs became like jelly. I buckled at the knees and collapsed like the proverbial 'rug was pulled from under my feet'. The thought of Tony experiencing this pain made me so weak, I just fell to the kitchen floor.

There was no way I could drive myself to the hospital; so my always staunch husband drove. After the suturing, we returned home and found a laugh emerging, first due to the sanitary napkin visualization and then because while sitting in the hospital waiting room, the hospital personnel asked questions about Tony's state of mind, they were very concerned that maybe slitting his wrist may have been intentional. "A possible attempted suicide". Tod was our witness, this was not the case it was a true accident and Tony's comment was "if I wanted to end it all, I would not have botched up the job". What a true statement this eventually turned out to be.

Back to Tony's new zest for this new found sport of skiing and the fact that Gina's husband, Bob was raised in Switzerland for twelve years and, of course, due to the environment in itself was very conducive for everyone to learn to ski. Bob took Gina on many ski trips and even with her physical impairment, she held her own. Tony was now their tag-along, and now added skiing to his repetoire of sport outings.

My husband and I being supportive, but not necessarily enthusiastic about this new sport, pondered over the idea of finding a cabin in the Catskills, a place where the family would be able to go when they needed the weekend to get away. Finding a cabin in the Catskills would make it convenient for all of them to have a place to stay when going skiing.

In 1983, we searched for a perfect spot, not too close to the actual skiing resorts, for it would be too congested and certainly very expensive. We found a tract of acreage (five acres) on Thunder Hill in the town of Grahamsville, New York, twenty minutes from Bellaire Mountain and forty minutes from Hunter Mountain. The builder advertised the five acres with a wooden frame shell for a cabin. The electricity would be serviced to the outside of the house, the septic tank installed and a water well dug close to the house for easy access. The inside of the cabin was void of everything; the only structure was the four outside walls, a partial loft with a flimsy staircase included. What a venture we undertook, but we were younger and more able bodied, so after much deliberation, after days of discussion both separately and united, we made the great decision and found the assertiveness needed to proceed to purchase this cabin.

We instructed the builder to place the cabin in the rear of the property, one hundred feet from a seasonal descending gushing stream, which was not only picturesque, but convenient to haul water before we were able to install indoor plumbing. Of course, being a city person, the first accommodation had to be the bathroom. There was no way I would share the outdoors with whatever creatures would roam this piece of property. Keep in mind though, there was no electricity for us to use power tools, so everything we did was real *manual* labor. I was black and blue for months, but it was a challenge which we knew full well would entail hard strenuous hand labor. We eventually rented a gas generator and that helped speed up the interior construction. Every weekend we would pack up, tools in hand and full of energy and willingness to brave this monumental task. Most of the time we had the help of Gina and Bob and sometimes had the help from Tony, Jr. Keep in mind that Tony was a pencil pusher, a hammer was very foreign to him, but again, a family that works together, stays together. How beautiful it all seemed and it truly was at that time. We worked hard, enjoyed each other's company, ate as if there was no tomorrow, played board games in the evening, laughed a lot and accomplished wonders with this simple modest unadorned wooden secluded mountainous cabin.

Our first accomplishment was the quickly installed powder blue fully tiled bathroom, stall shower, vanity etc. At least we had some comforts of home, expeditiously, pronto, and posthaste. One by one all the essentials were installed, heating initially was partially from a wood burning pot belly stove installed over a brick platform with a brick fire wall in the back and the remainder of the heating from electric baseboard radiators. We could not use these radiators until after the electricity was installed, inspected and functional, which took about another two months. We do recall many freezing nights we all huddled together in sleeping bags on the floor trying to stay warm, waking up stiff from the cold and aching from sleeping on the hard floor, but we still found humor at the entire sight.

We next tackled the bedroom, this was quite simple compared to the other finished projects. The walls needed to be installed, insulated, secure the panels and violá instant sleeping quarters. The loft also contained space for additional beds. Two twin beds and two pull-out sleepers, we had enough sleeping space for eight guests. This was old hat now; we already had experience from the downstairs bedroom, that the upstairs bedroom was a cinch. The kitchen was installed with fully functional electric range, beautiful oak cabinets and a compact refrigerator. The comforts of home were not lacking in any way, shape or form. The entire house was then completely insulated and diagonal cedar planking installed to the peaked ceilings, a wood parquet floor was laid and almost magically the entire project was complete, functional and extremely beautiful. The magic part took a total of **one year** of weekends, vacations, holidays, etc.

After the entire interior project was completed, we now had to do some work on the outside, the perimeter of the cabin needed some landscaping. This was facilitated by the fact that there were a multitude of bushes and trees already there on the property, they were there for the taking and replacing them somewhere more conspicuous and enhancing. The front entrance needed imagination and guts. There were no stairs to ascend to reach the deck from the bottom of the incline the house was built on. We all scouted the area to find big pieces of slate that we could haul to make a rustic stone stairway. My husband, my son-in-law Bob and of course, my son Tony took the Volvo with the attached trailer and headed into the dense woods to find some perfect pieces of slate. The trailer was half way loaded and they were hoisting a very large section of slate when my husband shouted to Tony, "Please be careful, this piece is very heavy and I don't want you to get your hand caught under it." Tony's response, "Don't worry dad", no sooner said and horror strikes again. Tony managed to wedge his hand under this heavy stone and crushed one of his fingers on his left hand.

The three of them returned immediately to the cabin. I was out hauling some logs for the fire and when I entered the cabin I saw Gina's face, white as a sheet, with a frightened leer which I quickly understood that something was seriously wrong. Of course, the first aid kit was not nearly sufficient for what we were dealing with. Gina speedily washed his hand, analyzed the damage, quickly tore a sheet, wrapped Tony's hand the best she could and *demanded* he go to the nearest hospital for medical attention. Tony was *stubborn* and refused to go anywhere he did not readily know, so he opted to drive home to Kings Park so he could be tended to at St. John's in Smithtown.   By this time, Tony had friends in the emergency room and felt very comfortable there. This was his third E.R. venture. (Let's keep a tally)

It was Tony and I who drove home together, the remainder of the crew still needed to finish upstate and now you really should *try to visualize this scene.* Tony was driving with his left hand bandaged, bloodied and hurting outside the driver's window, straight up so he would not lose additional blood. I was sitting in the passenger seat, crying hysterically and praying we would get through the three- hour ride without further incident. That night, again, I shared the excruciating pain Tony was experiencing. We made it directly to St. John's in record time and again after the suturing, bandaging and administering of pain medication, we managed to laugh at the sight of him holding the injured third middle finger of his left hand out of the window, straight up and *imagine* no one gave him the gesture back.

As a young adult Tony constantly exhibited this zest for almost any physical challenge.   Even after he was out on his own, married, the main provider, the head of a household, the breadwinner, the pillar of his domain, the master of his castle, the next generation of Varleses, he still brought *me* years of worry. I did not get gray hairs at an early age due to heredity.   The unending worry when I knew he was still being the daredevil he grew into.   The times he would show me the bruises he had sustained from playing deck hockey. The livid black and blue bruises from the falls, the bangs, the tackles, the hurdles, etc. There were times when his shins were purple for weeks from these rough sports. I always interfered, I tried to suggest maybe he could find a sport less damaging, less hurtful. He would always laugh and his reply was always the same, "Life will always have pain and so remember this is part of life".   He felt he had made a commitment to being part of the team and would not and could not let them down. Rain or shine, Tony would be there, win or lose, he had to be a player. We viewed many a video that proved Tony's enthusiasm, his drive to be the 'best', his need to participate, his zest for live.

Part of all those challenges was Tony's quest for fulfillment of a task begun, succeeding and then joyously recounting the dangers, the pitfalls, the conquests, the wins, the joy of winning. He even relished in the recount of the agony of defeat. He participated and that was what was important. He was still growing, still conquering the unknown. If my son only knew that even though he was out of our home on his own, I still could not sleep knowing he was taking risks, riding the white water rapids, deep sea scuba diving and the like. And I use to think that playing football or softball was hurtful, little did I know. No matter what sport he was trying, he always gave his 100%, if not more. He gave his best, he gave his all. He put an enormous amount of energy into everything he attempted. This exuberant energy was certainly exercised also in his ambition, and goals in his professional life.

Digressing back to Tony being a junior at Kings Park High, his guidance counselor requested an interview/conference with us, his dad and me, and as we anticipated she related Tony's great achievements, scholastically. She reiterated the fact that he excelled in mathematics, which we were aware of, and of the devotion he gave to that subject. Tony was young when he realized what course of life he would take, he decided at an early age of thirteen, he would master in mathematics and conclude his higher education with a degree in Accounting and ultimately be a Certified Public Accountant. Again, true to his character, he pursued this career and succeeded. He graduated with honors, on May 13, 1984.

This was Tony's first employer. Getting out of college with a certificate, or a diploma doesn't necessarily get you a job. It opens the door, you walk through, and then reality takes over and above all you must prove yourself, you must perform exceptionally and brilliantly if you are to succeed. In the real business world it is not the ultimate of success just to obtain the job, one must excel in order to advance and prosper. As expected Tony did work hard, was well liked, received promotions accordingly and certainly felt he was on top of the world. Still, with all his success, he always remained caring and humble. Not to say when he received accolades he didn't 'flap those wings' and appeared to become cocky. Deep down though, I know his cockiness was a put on, a stage reflection, an attention getting device, his way of getting approval and recognition. The acknowledgment meant a lot to him.

Tony set goals both for himself and for the good of his family, so he needed to work overtime, his need to be an **overachiever** suddenly became an obsession. His quest for perfection became a fault and eventually his downfall. Looking back, I guess he stretched himself too thin, but even with all of this striving, he *seemed* to keep it all together.

His immediate family always came first. The balance of his family, us, his sister and her family, the clan of Uncles , Aunts, and Cousins, followed in rank of importance. All these Italians, who always loved to come together for feasts, holidays, and just plain everyday get-togethers, were the essence of what we believed in and how we were raised to respect, and honor our families. We received great joy from each other. Family did and always will mean a great deal to us. Our values were and are based on a wholesome family. That is why this tragedy becomes a nightmare, not solely for mom and dad, but an enclave of family. This enclave of family in a remote way certainly includes Tony's co-workers and the friends he made along the way.

The years at Margolin, Winer and Evans were very important, very pivotal, reflective and certainly the most impressive to us all, most notably to Tony.

Andy Daniels, one of Tony's closest co-worker and friend wrote this memoir about the adult Tony as follows:

"The first time I saw Tony was in the Staff room at the accounting firm we both worked for, *Margolin, Winer and Evans.* I had been working for the firm for about a year when I finally met Tony. He was traveling to Toronto a lot so he would not be in the office all that much. That first time I saw him (I should really say *heard* him), he and another staff member entered the quiet staff room with a bang. The two of them trampled into this sedate room like a cattle stampede.

The best impression I have of memorable moments were the conversations after our softball games. Tony would tell stories of the "tales of Toronto" and the humor was *how* the story was told, which was priceless and kept everyone in stitches. Our friendship grew around our humor, our interests and appreciation of each other's athletic abilities, **but most of all our work ethics.**

I later met Tony at the firm's softball games and practices. It was during and after the games that I came to know the personality that is uniquely TONY!

I would later travel at length with Tony to Toronto and our friendship grew stronger. I subsequently moved within ten minutes from where he lived and as we both got married and had families, our friendship grew even further. I left the accounting firm a year or so before Tony left. We often talked about his career and I think he appreciated my candor and opinion on what he was doing. We often spoke about having a private accounting practice together.

At work Tony was known as a *free thinker*. Many of his ideas were against the established grain, but usually turned out to be right on the mark. He gained the confidence of the Managing Partner of the firm. Teddy would give Tony a lot of leeway and freedom to work out his ideas. Tony's relationship with Teddy and his freedom intimidated many Managers and staff members that were of a higher rank. As a manager myself, when Tony was a senior accountant, I often heard other Managers comment on the inability to "control" Tony. As Tony's friend, I found these comments to be delightful, amusing and somewhat true.

Tony was a bulldog at work; he worked for the sake of finding the answer. He was driven with a capital D. He worked hours and hours each day and *always* with humor. We could work fourteen- hour days and I would enjoy it mainly due to working with him. He worked hard and played hard. We would work till 9:00 pm and then Tony would come up with the whimsical idea to go out and buy a Whiffle--ball and bat (which he would put on his expense account), we then would proceed to go play under the light of some office building in downtown Toronto till midnight. We would form teams during the day to play football after work. He would spend the day humorously taunting the other team into a frenzy. We would walk the streets after work and he would inevitably lead the way to finding every strange restaurant known to mankind.

He once found this unique German restaurant together with Steven Marks, another accountant from the firm. We ultimately ordered everything on the menu, which included frogs' legs, buffalo meat, pigeon, rabbit and venison. In of itself is not strange, but the fact that we ordered all of these items at the same time certainly was a feat.

The concept of international cuisine was initiated by Tony, we would order Sushi platters as big as pizza pie pans. We all had such a great time and an abundance of laughs as we engulfed it all. Tony once ate a scoop of wasiabi (the oriental hot stuff) just to see IF he could. We were all in total agreement that Tony's stomach was lined with lead.

The nights at Bardies Steak House, where Tony became the waiter's favorite customer, were the most memorable. Tony knew how to eat! We would order 'steak for two' for one. We could still see Tony as he drank an entire gravy bowl of hollandaise sauce just to make us laugh. We all **laughed with him**, not at him. All this eating was followed by Banana Flambé (Calories were not our major concern at that time). We would go to other restaurants but Tony would always insist we top the night off with the dessert at Bardies.

One night, Tony had the brilliant idea of going to each of the restaurants we frequented and just order our favorite dishes at each one. Off we went, eight or so accountants, led by Tony, to sample each delicacy from these establishments. Let me tell you, we got many a strange look. We once ate at a Russian restaurant at the top of the Sheraton Hotel. The restaurant was one of the best in the city and very exclusive. I remember Tony in his sweat pants, banging the domed silver serving covers together like cymbals while a couple next to us were celebrating their anniversary, they looked on in horror, but Tony quickly called the waiter and sent a bottle of champagne to their table.

I fondly recall Steven Marks (Snapper, Tony's nickname for him) and Tony once had an eating contest at a Sheraton buffet that had the whole table of ten accountants literally in tears from laughter. It was hilarious to watch and hear the comments as Tony taunted Steve. Guess who won the contest, Tony. Needless to say Tony gained a lot of weight while he traveled to Toronto, as did the rest of us. He was great at dubbing nicknames to the staff, just to get under their skin. His own nickname, *El Gordo*, I believe was self proclaimed and showed his good nature by not excluding himself from his own teasing."

- - * - -

The above episodes and escapades certainly showed Tony at his most carefree time and illuminates the personality of Tony always trying to make someone laugh. He proved his loved for friends, but most of all his love for life. Yes, Tony truly loved to eat which will be detailed in a later chapter, but his *sense of humor* was always remarkable and the one most common denominator again uniquely, Tony.

Andy also gave mention of Tony's sportsmanship and zeal, but to say that Tony would try his hand at many sports is an understatement. Whether he would excel or finish last (God forbid) was not the issue. It was the participation; the enthusiasm that precluded the events that was paramount to the task.

There is a specific incident I vividly and horrifyingly have a flashback of, it was sometime in 1991. Tony and several of his friends, Paul, Andy et al., became involved in the art of deep-sea scuba diving. This was a new venture for Tony and, of course, seemed very valuable to him at that time. There were several outings that he did well, he was a very avid and proficient swimmer, but the recollection I have was one particular weekend, Tony failed to surface in the proper time constraints.

At that time, I was working in Mod B-1 at Stony Brook Hospital as a secretary in the Internal Medicine Division and in walks Tony. He came to my unit to spare himself another trip to the emergency room. He resembled a monster from the "Deep Lagoon". It seems that he had surfaced ***too fast*** and ruptured the blood vessels in his eyes. He had striated blood in the orbital region of his head, forehead and the white part of his eyeballs were soaked a deep maroon red. You could not look at his face for more than ten seconds; it gave you the willies and goose bumps with your pore hairs standing on end. This was the typical symptom of someone with DT's.

I, of course, could not imagine why or how he found this sport entertaining. It was extremely dangerous, especially when one does not abide by the rules. But again, Tony thought he was invincible and non-destructible . ***So he did it his way.*** We spent that weekend talking to him with our faces turned down looking at the floor or looking up towards the ceiling. Tony found humor in the outcome of this escapade but vowed never to surface in such a manner to cause this freak he was looking at. He himself found it difficult to look at himself in the mirror. The zest for this sport also ebbed and Tony would, I was sure, continue to search for other daring adventures.

So I relate another, not so sane sport, in particular, white water rafting. Hanging in his bedroom right now is a picture featured in Chapter 4 , dated April 24, 1988. Of the five young men oaring down the rapids you can sharply see Tony's face squinting and straining to paddle the best, the hardest and the fastest. Seated up front, taking command and grimacing and probably under his breath yelling at his rowing mates to do better. I am sure it was not a contest, not a race, nor a competition, it was only that Tony needed to do the best he could, expected it from everyone else and he needed to "shine", and be able to make the unending statement "I Did it My Way".

On the opposite wall where the rafting photograph is displayed, very close to the entrance of his room, hangs the painting of "ZOSO", the logo and the emblem of Led Zeppelin Band. The naked winged man soaring into the puffy white smoky clouds amidst a sky of radiant blue.

In the years prior to his marriage, Tony had a voracious thirst to listen to the Led Zeppelin band, over and over until the music echoed throughout our home and certainly rebounded to the homes nearest to ours. If Tony saw "The Song Remains the Same" once he saw it at least twenty-two times. Would you say this was covetousness personified? I certainly had many comments to make regarding his need to idolize this heavy metal music band. Yet even to this day, there is something about the rendition of "Stairway to Heaven" that makes *me wonder.*

Last year, September 1999, our bereavement group from Massapequa participated in a project of having a "Survivors of Suicide" quilt put together in honor of our lost loved ones. The square was12" x 12" and was to be created, decorated, adorned, memorialized any way we wished. The obvious, and the design most widely used was a square with the picture of your loved one in the center with his/her name and perhaps words that symbolized or characterized that son, daughter, husband, wife, mother, father, aunt, uncle or any other relative or friend you wished to remember. My square consisted of Tony's latest family picture, with another photograph of him swinging his golf club, the emblem of the Kansas City Chiefs, and, of course, the immortalized words of "Our Angel", his date of birth and his date of death.

On the other square, Gina who is extremely talented and a fantastic artist in her own right, replicated the Led Zeppelin logo of the nude winged man soaring again into the sky. Gina had, when Tony was fifteen years of age, painted the exact image (pictured on page 49) on one of his denim jackets that he was reluctant to take off even when I needed to wash it.

Gina spent months hand painting this logo in finite detail, but she knew how much Tony idolized this scene, so she artistically and willingly crafted this for her brother.

Now, when it came time for Gina to participate in the quilt project, she again willingly consented to duplicate the winged man on her donated square. This time she added the words: "Once again, Only for You". When she had done the original jacket back in 1977, all Tony's friends requested a jacket just like his. Gina refused to paint the same scene, but she did do others, i.e. Van Halen, etc., but left Led Zeppelin strictly for her brother. He was so proud then and I am sure he is similarly happy now when he saw her latest work of art.

This quilt was made for our group, with the stipulation that we must share it five times a year with SPAN (Suicide Prevention Advocacy Network). They will travel around the states to display these quilts in the hopes of bringing suicide awareness to a higher level. At the time we presented the quilt to the Capital representatives, there were fifty quilts on the lawn in full display one could see so much sadness went with each and every one of the quilts, with each and every square, and the tears we shed I am sure would have sunk a myriad of ships. The heartbreak of eyeing the young, elderly, females, males, teenagers, service people, people of all walks of life, people of every ethnic denomination, people of every race, people of wealth, those from poverty, there is no immunity when it comes to dealing with this dreadful disease.

I recently attended a Suicide Prevention Conference and in a small workshop of Mothers who had lost an adult child, there was a mother who stated "I need to respect my daughter's decision that she felt it necessary to end her life". This mother somehow did not wish to identify her daughter's actions to be related to a mental illness. This mother found it difficult to imagine that a bright, beautiful, loving child with no symptoms of any irrationality may have harbored a mental disorder. My story related to this mother because neither did my son's personality ever indicate there could possibly be a mental imbalance that would cause such a drastic culmination of his life. I did not agree with her logic to respect her daughter's decision. A concept I find difficult to accept.

There are some people who feel I am obsessed with Tony's death. On the contrary, I feel more obsessed with his life. What he left behind. Those successes he would have achieved. His goals, his aspirations all went by the wayside. Yet, it needs to be said that this was a human being worthy of recognition, a decent, trustworthy buddy, an asset to whomever he befriended and certainly a precious son, brother, nephew, cousin. It goes without saying he was a loving husband and a responsible, conscientious and loving devoted father. He was a dependable, ideal, reliable, conscientious hard worker to each and every one of his employers. A very respectful relative to his entire out-reaching ethnic family. I cannot, in all good conscience, keep his life to myself. This would certainly be selfish on my part. I find the need to share his life and try to keep the memory of his existence active and kept stored in the archives of one's mind whenever and wherever possible.

Death is the culmination of one's existence. I think ahead and question was my own life worthwhile? Was I just a passing individual? Was I just a blasé person? Was I thriving? Was I of use to someone? Was I so nonchalant that I would not be mentioned? I cannot in all honesty do any less for my son.

My epilogue will include further discussion on mental illness in itself, its manifestations, consequences and the help that is definitely necessary and the strives the public, the researchers, the survivors, the health professionals are making in the education, awareness and the approaches needed to bring the alarming statistics to a minimum.

MY SON MY SON

Our arms are wrapped around you,
    although we are apart.
The tears have not diminished,
    nor the pain without hearts.

Your presence will always linger,
    deep within our souls.
The love we always shared,
    forever we will hold.

Son, please remember,
    that day will surely come,
When we are all together,
    that day we'll see the sun.

How can one such person,
    who brought us so much joy,
Knowing your were our special son,
    now left us with such a void.

The darkness now encumbered,
    your smile did bring us light.
Your kindness is remembered,
    your memories held on tight.

Mom and Dad

CHAPTER SIX

I ONLY HAVE EYES FOR YOU

> *Are the stars out tonight?*
> *I don't know if it's cloudy or bright*
> *Cause, I only have eyes for you, dear.*

Recollections are sometimes happy, sometimes sad, sometimes unusual, sometimes strange, but most of all they are the images that last throughout one's lifetime. There are those times where the images reflect one another.

When I recall Tony as a toddler, one of those images now appears sharply as I look back and see him, he was about two years old, in fact, it was the day President John F. Kennedy was assassinated, November 22, 1963. Tony sat with me watching television and asked why I was crying. I tried to explain, but he was too young to comprehend death. All he really knew was mommy was sad and he looked very puzzled when he saw the tears streaming down my face. How ironic thirty-four years and five days later those same tears surged down my face, only this time my son was not by my side physically, he was not there to hold my hand and look up at me with those woeful eyes he had at times when he was perplexed. Spiritually, I am sure he walked me through the most horrendous day of my life, November 27, 1997. The day my life ended with his. Why wasn't he there remembering the sorrow I had for a stranger? Was he shedding his own tears that day? When we discovered his body, his dad and I, I saw what looked like tears on his cheeks and the saddest expression anyone could ever imagine on a face that was always so very full of smiles. Oh! My Son, My Son!

In the summer of 1997, August 30th, only three months prior to that excruciating pain I suffered by his death, Tony again watched me cry and wipe those tears for even another stranger. The death of Princess Diana, who had died in that horrible accident.   Again the same question, this time from an adult, "Mom, why do you get so sad? How come you get so emotional? How can you cry for someone you don't even know? How would you ever handle the death of someone you know and love?" Was Tony questioning me for *real answers* or simply trying to comprehend how emotional I could be? I'll never know.

Let us reflect back to happier times:

Before Tony met the love of his life, my mom and I tried so hard to find him a "nice little Italian girl", the accent is on the Italian.

In 1984 Tony was living in Long Island City with my mom, to be closer to New York City, nearer to work in Manhattan, so that the commuting wouldn't take so long. My mom lived on Vernon Blvd. and Jackson Avenue, one subway stop from Grand Central Station. The year and one-half he lived with his grandmother was a very trying time for both her and Tony. She couldn't comprehend Tony's odd and long work hours and he couldn't understand why she needed to worry so much. She worried about him constantly. This was my mom, there was no changing her, she did it to me and now renewed her anxieties with Tony. Here you can find the familiar trait, always worrying, always fearing the worse.

Tony had one salvation, he became close to the Tiseo family, they were close friends of my mom and also tenants in her other building, in Long Island City. I didn't quite understand the friendship at first since Pietro and Lina were old enough to be his parents, but here again Tony seemed to fit in just perfectly.

Here are some of the Tiseo Family 's memories of Tony

From Pietro:

"Tony was like a son to me. I would always look forward to him coming over and I constantly asked his grandmother, whom we called Zia (Aunt) Rosina, 'When is Tony coming so I could have some prosciutto (Italian cured ham) ready for him. Tony loved prosciutto.

Every time Tony came over, prosciutto was there for him and we would put the dish in front of him and loved to watch him enjoy the meal. I would always ask Tony when he was going to find a nice girl and he would always respond, 'Pietro, le femine sono tutte puttane' (Ladies are tramps), (a literal translation, but common verbiage in the Italian language). I would always laugh uncontrollably.

The one thing I know for sure the days that I spent with Tony will always be remembered, he knew how to brighten up our home."

From Lina:

"After our meals Tony and I would sit at the table and talk about his family, his background, his work, etc. Tony was always so proud to tell us stories and memories of his maternal grandfather Rocco. Every time he talked about his parents and his sister Gina his eyes lit up with pride."

From Domenick and Anthony - The Tiseo Sons:

"We remember Tony's love for softball and a few times we went to Long Island with him to play softball. We always had such a great time."

_ _*_ _

My husband and I were so grateful to the Tiseo family for taking Tony under their wing while he was living with my mother. It was nice he had someone to talk to, (they spoke English), Tony had someone to joke with, someone to reminisce with, and especially the fact that I conjured up a beautiful scenario that maybe one day Tony and Betty, their youngest daughter, would somehow hit it off and have a more involved serious relationship. God's ordinance did not allow this to happen, and Lina and I were both saddened by the outcome. I know now, my life may have had a different sequel had this been the outcome. We bowed to God's holy will and accepted the disappointment, for I was always a true believer of fate and what is in store for the future comes from Him and there is nothing on earth someone can do to change this tapestry. Disappointment does give way to logic and so their friendship continued, flourished and culminated also on that dreadful day. The Tiseo family still have beautiful memories of Tony and they wish to share the following in his tribute:

From Tina Conti, The Tiseo's eldest daughter:

Tina was the eldest of the four Tiseo children and, of course, she remembers Tony the most. *Tina recalls:*

"It was June 18, 1985, I was pregnant with my second child, Lisa Marie, and I was due for a caesarian section so I went to the hospital the night before ..... but before going to the hospital, we dropped off our son Anthony, who was 2 1/2 years old at the time, to my parents' home. It was about 7:00 pm and Anthony had a little car, it looked like a race car, one that you pedal. It was his favorite thing. He was riding it and then he saw Tony pull up into the driveway and was talking to Tony a mile a minute about his new race car. He wanted to race with Tony.

Tony got into his Monte Carlo and went slowly down the street as my son Anthony raced on the sidewalk.......he was thrilled and, of course, Tony let him win. When he got out of the car Tony picked Anthony up in his arms and said 'Yeah, you're the winner!!!!'. Then Tony looked at Anthony very seriously and said 'Anthony it is fun to race, but remember a car is a weapon, it can be very dangerous'. My son Anthony is now seventeen and he still remembers the race and TONY."

Tina further recalls that "one day we went to Sunken Meadow Beach and had a picnic. I brought the game Trivia Pursuit. Well, Tony and me were in a head to head competition. We were competing as if we were going to win a million dollars. At the end no one wanted to play with us because they said Tony and me were annoying and should play alone. I asked Tony 'are we annoying?', he said 'no way, they're all just jealous!'".

- - * - -

Tony always seemed to fit in with every age group. He would sit and talk for hours with his grandparents, his aunts and uncles and all my foreign speaking cousins. Even though conversation may have been difficult due to the language barrier, Tony managed to use hand signs as all Italians do and converse the best he could. Young or old Tony always made them feel comfortable. Of course, without saying, he fit in best with people his own age.

Betty Barone, Pietro's youngest daughter was a few years younger than Tony and she was the one my mom and I were trying to fix him up with. Betty remembers Tony with a lot of respect. Betty did, at that time, have a boyfriend Matt (whom she eventually married) so Tony being "Mr. Nice Guy" did not wish to intrude on their relationship. My mom and I tried very hard, even to the point of arguing with Tony and getting him upset, but he had integrity and he certainly was a gentleman and a man of honor. Tony would never do anything so under handed or sly to split Betty and Matt up. He respected Betty as a very very close friend, and of course, without saying he respected her family and would not have wanted to hurt any of them in any way. He would say to me "Let God do His work, whatever will be, will be". Sometimes when I became insistent, he would shout "mind your business". This was a phrase that he certainly repeated several times during those years.

Betty Barone's great memories of Tony:
Betty recalls Tony's visits vividly and here are a few excerpts she shared with us:

"Some nights at the Tiseo house things were a little boring, especially summer nights, but when Tony pulled up in the driveway, I knew the party was about to begin.

Since Tony and I had a little crush on each other it especially made things more exciting. His grandmother would call to tell me that he had confided in her that he loved when I wore pink, so I made it a point that whenever I knew he was coming over, I wore PINK......

I specifically remember one night when Tony and his grandmother came to visit, we had just finished having coffee so, I was in the kitchen washing the cups (like a good Italian girl would) and Tony, of course, said 'let me help wash the cups' and so he did, but he washed them with scorching hot water and said 'see, now they are not only clean, but sterilized'. We laughed so much that night and from then on, every time my mom told me to wash the cups, I would say 'call Tony'.

The times I would always make a big deal about how important my dolls were to me but Tony would say 'you're too old to play with dolls' and we would have a debate over if I was too old for dolls or not, but as usual any subject would set up a debate with Tony.(Just for laughs) Well, one night I went to bed and when I looked up I saw two of my dolls dangling on the cord of the Venetian blind ....this is when I knew Tony would rather win the debate or else. Once again, I silently laughed."

Betty continues to recall that "one night a friend of mine was at my house and we were just listening to music, not having anything else to do......we saw Tony pull up and I quickly said 'hey, let's ask Tony to take us for ice cream' .....Well he said NO!..... (Of course, he was kidding) and lucky for us his grandmother was there and she INSISTED 'porta queste ragazze per il gelato!!!' (Take these girls for ice cream!!!) And so he did. The whole way there and all the way back home we had a blast with the radio on and us singing our heads off!!!.

I always thought of Tony as a very special person. He would light up a room with his Smile and this is the memory we ALL have of him ....**His Smile.**"

- - * - -

Flashback to 1986:

Recalling, looking back to the year 1986 -   Rushing through the front door one evening in November, Tony came in shouting: "She's the one, I found my soul-mate, I found the woman I am going to grow old with, the wonderful girl I wish to spend the rest of my life with, the vision of my dreams, the future mother of my children. The gift that God sent to me personally. Oh! How happy I will be".

Being the generous person he was, my son's first thoughts were "what beautiful gifts could I shower upon this girl of my dreams". Tony would not question the price of the object, in as much as he wished to bestow the best he could to someone he cared for and loved, whether it was his family or friends. He scouted the jewelry stores for the perfect gift and ultimately decided on a pendant of a heart with one carat of diamonds. Diamonds because they were precious and a heart to signify his love. The pendant, at that time, was a unique one. It has since become a very popular piece of jewelry since it was and still is a beautiful item. When Tony arrived home with the necklace, he sparkled as much as the diamonds did.

His enthusiasm and his joy were very hard to contain. He had this unique smirk on his face when he felt he had accomplished something special, but his eyes told the whole story more vividly. He gleamed and glowed with utter excitement.

Tony could not wait for all of us to meet his perfect mate, this wonderful creature of God. She was welcomed and accepted immediately into our family. We considered ourselves lucky that this girl melded so nicely into our family, she never seemed to criticize our family's closeness, and she seemed to understand our cultural background. There was a cohesiveness that was widely accepted by our entire family, both the immediate and the distant ones. Our son asked if it would be possible for the 'love of his life' to move into our spare guest room, or rather to utilize our daughter's room, which was still intact since she had married in 1978. His girl had no place to go, her plans to move in with girlfriends fell through, and so we received and welcomed her as a guest. To say we treated her like a daughter is an understatement.

Was I jealous that Tony was replacing me as the love of his life? It may have seemed so, but believe me, as truthful as I can be Tony was not a mama's boy. By no stretch of the imagination. I was ecstatic that he had found his soul mate and would settle down. I knew he would make someone a good husband and I had no doubts that he would make a fantastic father. I was pleased that he wanted to get married, buy a home, have a family, and do all the things that parents pray for and have my dreams come true. Tony had enough love in his heart to be able to share with me. "A man must leave his family if he is to carry on and succeed. The bible states 'and the two of them shall become one' and so it is written, so it is done."

I was always pleased that Tony, as a son, treated me so well and I knew he would do the same as a husband. There was no competition, just sharing. I couldn't do enough for them both. My son did shower me with the most exciting and unusual gifts, my favorites, my special color, lavender, but I always knew I was second in his life.

I always appreciated immensely that Tony went out of his way to find the most unique gift and I would anticipate the look on his face when I opened his thoughtful and thought out special presentation. Nothing gave him the greatest of pleasure.

The winter of 1985, he was still a junior member of the firm of Margolin, Winer and Evans, but he was doing well and was well liked and showed a very promising future with the firm. Tony wished to, most of all, show his appreciation to us for helping him through his college years, with free room and board, paid tuition, paid extra curricula activities, gave him his new car an Oldsmobile Firenza for graduation and so his ideal gift for me that Christmas was a full length mahogany mink coat. Where was I going to wear such an extravagant adornment? It didn't matter, he considered it something every mom should have and so there he was in the fur salon at Macy's purchasing this exquisite apparel for me to make my Christmas the biggest and brightest ever. Now, I had to think of where to wear this beautiful coat. The opera? Broadway shows? I never did any of those things. So, whatever possessed him to think this was a practical gift, I'll never understand. Fifteen years later, I must admit, I now wear this coat with pride and I wear it every chance I get. Not just the special occasions. Besides it being very warm, it will never wear out, it will never go out of style and I always feel his arms wrapped around me every time I put this coat on my shoulders. The warmth generated is not only from the coat itself, but also from the intentions and memories that encompassed this most special loving gift.

Every birthday, every Mother's Day, every Easter, every Anniversary, you could rest assured that Tony would present with the appropriate magnificent special gift imaginable. He would go out of his way to pick my favorite color, styles he knew I would prefer, not necessarily the most expensive (though sometimes it was very expensive), the money was never an issue, but the selection was well thought out and always appropriate and stylish. The silk blouses, the terry robes, the Lord & Taylor fashionable handbag, the silk scarves with matching gloves. The list goes on and on. One Christmas the doorbell rang, when I opened the door there stood P.C. Richards delivery man with a large screen console television and a note from Tony "Merry Christmas Mom and Dad". He later got even more creative with theater tickets to top Broadway plays, and without saying he always managed the best seats available. Even the trip to England he gave us in 1995 as a 39th Wedding Anniversary gift, he made sure there were theater tickets at the London Palladium to see the ever-popular "Oliver".

CHAPTER SEVEN

TONIGHT I CELEBRATE MY LOVE FOR YOU

This day will be a start
of many more to come.
Filled with joy and "love"
That's where it started from.
How perfect it would be,
if everyday were filled,
With today's unending "love",
it would, if it could be willed.

But just remember this
That "love" will overcome.
And overlook your differences
When trying times are done.
The sad times, if there may be,
The good times will surpass.
Together you should have,
A "love" that will surely last.

How can we folks go on?
We're sharing such a 'Son'.
The "love" we always gave you,
The times we had such fun.
We embrace another child,
We're sure will fit in fine.
To share our "love" with someone else,
And she to us in time.

May sunshine be yours the years ahead,
And your future be always bright.
As your beginnings now will start,
With all our "love" to make it right.
Mom and Dad

That poem I wrote on the morning of their wedding day, July 9, 1988. Words that were written from the bottom of my heart, in true sincerity and with as much "love" anyone could wish on their children. I always shared similar poetic words with my children because I truly felt they were, and still are, 'the most important part of my life.' Is it only an Italian idiosyncrasy to want to shower your children with everything that was lacking in your own life, to shower them with as much 'love' anyone could possibly give, or is this an international, universal parental wish? I'm sure it is the latter.

Tony's wedding and reception was the typical Italian celebration. Lots of friends, a multitude of relatives, plenty of food and drink (emphasis on the food). The matrimonial sacrament was consecrated by Mgr. John Maurer, my son-in law's uncle, who has since departed from this earth. Mgr. Maurer was a prodigious person, an awe-inspiring individual and a magnificent role model. Mgr. Maurer was well liked and is sorely missed by so many. He officiated not only at Tony's ceremony, but also at any and all of our family and religious functions, weddings, christenings, communions, confirmations, etc. That particular year St. Joseph's Church in Kings Park did not have the date available for the wedding ceremony, so we scouted several of the churches within our area and was fortunate enough that St. Francis Assisi Church in Greenlawn had an opening for the day we requested. Of course, the closest friends were in the bridal party, starting with Billy Nicholson (Tony's lifetime pal) officiated as his best man, the ushers were: John Nicolette (college buddy), Tod Skidmore (teenage friend and co-worker from Pathmark), Tony Nigro (co-worker from Margolin, Winer and Evans), Joe Bublé (also a co-worker from M.W. & E.), and Ben Neadom (his future brother-in-law). The men wore the classic pale gray tuxedos and I swear they were the most handsome group of gentlemen you would ever want to set your eyes upon. (Again, I may be a slight bit prejudiced, but who will try to dispute my opinion). The bridesmaids wore the most stunning medium shaded lavender sateen gowns, simple but elegant.

The bridesmaids included: Nikki Tomesck (bride's best friend and college classmate) was the maid of honor, Gina Maurer (Tony's sister), Natalie Marszak (bride's college classmate),Cathy Pitts (bride's future sister-in-law), Terry (Tony's Nigro's wife), and Roberta Baker (Joe Bublé's fiancé.)

The reception was held at The Larkfield Manor in Northport, the usual extravagant buffet cocktail hour, the four hour six course dinner and the spectacular (best part of the evening) Viennese table. Everything I mentioned was certainly beautiful and delicious, but what impressed all the guests the most was the closeness of all his friends from every stage of Tony's life to the present day. There was so much gaiety, so much laughter, everyone stated they wished the night would never end.

During the evening, Tony and Billy came up to the microphone and belted out several of their childhood routines, they even tried to replicate their soft shoe steps, but somehow it wasn't quite as cute as when they were toddlers. Nonetheless, Tony's wedding day was memorable for all who attended and I can still see myself crying while I was dancing with him to "Sunrise, Sunset". As I have continuously noted, I was and still am very emotional, to say the least. They were tears of joy when I danced with my son that evening. Without a doubt the sun did rise with him and little did I know the sun would set with him, so soon, so untimely, so tragically.

What really tugged at your heartstrings was Tony dancing with his grandmother (My mom). They adored each other. There was no concealing their closeness and their love for one another. A very sad note to interject, 'on the day we found Tony's body, he was holding the picture of himself and his grandmother dancing at the wedding, he had this picture resting in his left hand. The remainder of the album had been opened up and the pictures lay on the front seat of the car. Another album also open and lay on the passenger seat was that of his family. What was Tony trying to tell us that day? Was he conveying the fact that he would be joining his grandmother soon? Was he saying good bye to his family?. The flashbacks of those horrendous specific images of that dreadful day are very much still present today. These effigies haunt me in the daytime and certainly when I am trying to sleep at night. Oh! these ongoing tortuous nightmares. Sleep is one thing that has become very disjointed. We should be grateful that Morpheus takes over at the very beginning of the tragedy to numb one's senses to mask what has occurred. While you sleep, time flits by, but yet time never passes in your grief. You awake to find your ache, your pain, your hurting is still very much acute and present. The nights are filled with tossing and turning, then reality sets in, the unending torture of the thought that you will never see your loved one again, at least not in this world, continues to present itself over and over again.

Here is when you begin to pray your own world should end, so that maybe you will encounter that part of you that has crossed over. You begin to want to leave behind the fun, the gaiety, and the laughter you hear surrounding yourself. How can there be any joy left in such sorrowful times? Over and over again, the repertoire is the same. The longing to sleep, but normal sleep just does not exist. Will it ever?

When my mom died in 1994 (September 2), we somehow acknowledged that her illness, (gastric carcinoma) would have caused her months, maybe even years of pain. We gripped our emotions and succeeded in relinquishing to God's holy will. After the initial shock of death, the realization of the finality of her life, which we felt now may have been a blessing in disguise. She was not the type of person who could or would have coped with the seriousness of cancer and the long hard battle that would have ensued in conquering the treatments which sometimes leave a person in more pain than the illness itself. The chemotherapy, the radiation, we know for a fact she would not have tolerated either both physically or emotionally. We, the family, banded together and forged on with the knowledge that mom was at rest and at peace, with no pain. She was in the arms of the Lord and would be watching over all of us. My mom is sorely missed, for she was the matriarch, our tower and our strength. She was also our sounding board, and sometimes even our adversary. Several times she was (at least mine) our enemy; when I refused to cower to her eccentricities. She relentlessly chastised me for moving fifty miles away from her and that it took at least a minimum of an hour to get to Long Island City from where we were living in Kings Park. When we first moved to Kings Park in 1973 she refused to speak to me, kept her silence for four months. Then my dad became very ill and there was the need for me to chauffeur him back and forth to the hospital and doctors and that priority became greater than her pride.

Myself, my husband, my daughter, my son-in-law, but especially my son had a relationship with my mother that reflected respect, honor and mostly love for this woman whose life centered on us. We were her life and my prayers today, are prayers of gratefulness to God that she pre-deceased the love of her life and the love of my life, my only son, Tony. There were several times when Tony disputed whom Grandma loved more, him or Gina, I tried to convince him that he was her hero, her pride and joy. In fact, many times Tony defended her with all his might when we found it necessary to contradict her actions and infractions that she was too stubborn to concede to. She felt she was always right in her mind no matter what the discussion, her stubbornness was a great fault of hers, but she was 'the boss' and we, especially Tony, would let her win the battle and ultimately the war. Because we all *LOVED* her.

My mom's greatest joy was when she would shower us with gifts, the more festive the occasion, the bigger, the more elaborate the gift. I believe this trait must be where Tony inherited his "giving" genes. When I was married in 1956 (June 2), my mom and dad gave us, among other gifts, a 1956 pink Cadillac (Wow!). The long slender rear fenders made this a classical car. They even wrote a song about the pink Cadillac. The song wasn't written for us, it was released years after we were married. But this car was certainly the cat's meow. We were the envy of our small community in Long Island City. The first couple ever to receive such an extravagant gift.

And so, it became a tradition that my parents would shower my children with the same elaborate gift. On Gina and Bob's wedding day, much to their surprise they received from their grandparents a white and maroon Chrysler Cordoba. Ricardo Montelban didn't have to advertise this automobile because we fell in love with it immediately and so did my daughter and her new husband. This was in 1978 and then exactly ten years later it was Tony's turn. This time, since cars were more expensive, it was not wise to surprise someone without making sure it was their dream car, so we asked Tony and his fiancé to pick the car of their choice. They opted for a Mercury Cougar, white with a navy blue carriage top. Tony was proud of their car but most of all proud to be the grandson whom my mom adored. My dad was not fortunate to be here when Tony married, he had passed away in 1981, but we knew deep in our hearts that he was looking down at Tony and his bride and smiling at the gift he would have purchased had he been here. My dad always teased Tony that he was a true Varlese, not an Evangelista like himself, but Tony had a unique grin that was the same as my dad when he was proud of doing something special. Maybe it was a small smirk, but it was a unique grin that both my dad and Tony shared when giving of themselves.

-- * --

Love comes in many forms, a mother and father's love to nurture, provide, teach, make sure a child is healthy, educated enough to make something of themselves, so they would be self-sufficient. Parents raise their children to have integrity, be decent people and above all have respect for themselves and others.

Love comes from a child for their parents, siblings, childhood school friends, neighborhood friends and a special kind of love for their minuscule possessions. Toys, games, and sports equipment may also fall into this category.

Love for your future mate at first begins with physical attraction, then a chemical attraction where an adult relationship blossoms into a sexual, passionate, overwhelming starry eyed, bell ringing and a 'I can not live without you' feeling. This love flourishes when two people give of themselves, 100%. The relationship becomes one of honor, cherishing and understanding. They learn to cope with the ups and downs, the good times and the bad times. So where or when does love go wrong?

Love then comes a true full circle, when your child now has a child of his own and the cycle repeats and repeats itself. The creation of life, the nurturing and fulfillment of God's plan.

Tony's vow of 'till death us do part' meant so much to him . He professed his love on the altar of God , for better or worse, richer or poorer, in sickness and in health, and these vows were sacred. The week before his death he verbally repeated these vows to me. Should I have picked up on something he was trying to tell me? Was I so dense? My heart was open but now I question whether my brain was being receptive to the underlying conversations we were having during those weeks he was falling into his deep, dark, depression.

When Tony loved, he loved hard. There was no mediocre way for him to love. He loved with his heart and soul. To some it may seem that these are only words, but I, his closest confidante, knew him best and it was I who spent the last days with him, listening, cuddling him, watching him cry and it was I who hugged him close to my heart when I heard him vow how much he loved his wife and children. Remember it was I who carried this child for nine months and now it was I who had to watch him revert back to that infant where he needed to cry and have me clutch him closely.

Tony had a knack to be powerful, sometimes to a fault, I remember back to 1995 and his trip to Kansas City. Tony was obsessed with the "Chiefs", to say the least. Besides the tremendous joy he obtained from playing golf with his co-workers and friends on Saturday mornings, he exerted an enormous amount of exuberance when it came to the Kansas City Chiefs football team. Why or how they were his favorite football team only he would be able to convey. He avidly tried not to miss any of their televised games and he even found true disappointment when they were defeated. When they **won** a game, Eugene Drive knew it immediately; one could hear Tony's shouts of exhilaration and excitement.

In September 1995 Tony was able to travel to Kansas City and be a first hand spectator . His trip to the Arrowhead Stadium was one he quoted "a trip I will never forget". The hustle and bustle of actually being there physically gave Tony a true rush. This particular Sunday the Chiefs were playing against the Oakland Raiders, and whether the Chiefs won or lost they would always be the greatest team in Tony's mindset. The only thing I see clearly about this trip was when he returned home he presented his family, especially his sons with every Kansas City Chief memorabilia that anyone could imagine. There were the blankets, the marble wall plaque, the banners, the sweatshirts, the caps, the glassware, the posters, etc. I don't think he missed any type of souvenir they were selling. It was enough to see the brightness on Tony's face when he returned home with all these gifts for his family. Of course, I commented that he was eccentric and was immediately put in my place by his usual remark, "Mom, you are so old-fashioned, I can't give my sons enough". For any one to understand this is very difficult, but knowing Tony the way I did, I may be the only one who does understand. Did the means justify the end? Hardly!

PROUD DAD

"Mom, I am walking on cloud nine again", Tony remarked on January 12, 1991. (Reference of the first time he made the statement was on July 9, 1988). You see, January 12, 1991 was when his first-born had arrived at St. John's Hospital in Smithtown. Tony rushed to buy the biggest, I mean *huge*, four-foot powder blue plush teddy bear. Together with the dozen red long stem American beauty roses, and a catcher's mitt. With the teddy bear and balloons attached, Tony proceeded to greet his precious first-born son, with royalty treatment bar none. He gave his son his own name because he now was doubly proud, he had his dad's name, and proud to follow in his dad's footsteps, proud of his heritage, proud of his legacy, proud of his family, proud to pass this on to his first born. He also very proudly gave Anthony a second name, Rocco, to honor and respect his deceased maternal grandfather's name. He knew Nonna (my mom) would be ecstatic that Tony honored grandpa. I decidedly mentioned that it was a very ethnic name and maybe he should reconsider, but Tony didn't care. He respected this tradition and thought it would be a great honor to his grandpa and so he did not listen to anyone. He knew how much grandma would love having Anthony named after her husband.

In retrospect, Rocky was not an apropos name for a very sensitive, very shy, very slight, very fair skinned, very blond haired child. I truly hope and pray Anthony accepts his middle name with the love and respect it was given him. In describing Anthony, his first born, he seems to be the mirror image of his father as a child. Tony had blond hair, fair skinned, and was very shy and sensitive. Tony, like Anthony, had a quiet demeanor, yet he knew what he wanted and would aspire in due time.

Proud Dad Once Again

The scenario of roses, the plush four foot, this time it was brown, teddy bear was replayed step by step, inch by inch. Catcher's mitt and balloons, etc. were strung from door to door. Tony, by no means, would want to slight his second son in any way. Always while growing up, Tony would sometimes make snide remarks about him being second to his sister and would infer he was side stepped being the second child, so he himself was careful not to make Nicholas second to Anthony. They were both equal, both precious, both the same, and yet both different. The same in love and caring, the same in attention, the same in recognition, and yet different as night and day in that their personalities were so opposite.

Three years later, February 14, 1994, Tony's second son arrived. It was not unusual or surprising that I, as a grandma, wished a daughter for him. I visualized a perky, bubbly, pigtailed, spunky ringlet blond, but in God's wisdom it was not meant to be. Even though Nicholas Alexander, Tony's second child, did not turn out to be a girl, we welcomed and loved him just as much. Needless to repeat, Tony was again another proud peacock.

Nicholas was given a second name, Alexander. Tony and his wife knew I had a deep preference to the name Alexander, it may have been a sense of royalty that I subconsciously harbored, but it happened to be a name I really liked. Again, in acknowledgment and in respect for me, Nicholas received his second name. Tony had a quirky name for his second son, he used to call him 'Whistle', why he gave him this nickname, he never really told us.

Nicholas was born three months after my first granddaughter. On November 3, 1993 Gina gave birth to Kerrin Rose, her second name was given to honor my mom. We seemed to have such a perfect family, and we knew we were blessed to have such beautiful healthy grandchildren. To say we were all on cloud nine is an understatement.

Acknowledging respect for the family Tony and his wife desired that Gina and her husband Bob be godparents to Nicholas. Gina was also godmother to Anthony, which was suggested by Tony's wife, since she had requested her brother to be the godfather for Anthony. It seemed appropriate that brother and sister from each side of the family should be selected for such a great honor of being godparents to God's beautiful creation.

Our family was so happy, so perfect at this point of our lives. The children were doing well, the grandchildren were healthy, happy and most of all loved. As a family tradition, Kerrin and Nicholas were christened at the same time, at the same church, St. Joseph's in Kings Park. Tony and his wife were godparents for Kerrin. We celebrated in a very elaborate manner at the Larkfield Manor. Since Tony's wedding was held there, we knew the affair would be a beautiful one and very exceptional.

Those were the happiest of times. This very close knit family made sure all the holidays, birthdays, anniversaries, special celebrations were carried out in a special way. Of course, due to our ethnic background, being Italian, food and drink were always in abundance and always very essential. We all loved to share our happy times, our memorable times with relatives and friends. Our world revolved around our family, the traditions, the participation in the festivities, both the elaborate ones and the intimate ones, they were all very special and always very thought out.

I guess, outwardly the world was our oyster. It still was, until October 1997, when this perfect world crumbled beneath our feet. Our perfect family torn apart and shattered into a thousand slivers of glass likes the tumbling of a crystal wineglass hitting a concrete pavement. Our lives torn to shreds like a sheet of parchment fed through a most powerful shredder. Our hopes, our dreams scattered to the four corners of the world, like a cyclone hitting the sandy dunes on a desert beach. Like the eruption of a volcano spewing its lava on a beautiful terrain; reducing it to a mass of ashes and black smoldering lava and creating an ebony crater of pure ugliness.

From October 10, 1997 through November 27, 1997, my son was no longer the person we recognized. Our son who would have confronted any problem head-on, our son who accepted adversity and tried to revert it into something positive, our son who would have smiled at ill luck and find some good could come from it, our son who gave courage to anyone who needed comfort, our son who gave strength to weakness, our son was here no longer.

Where had my strong hero gone? His tears, his pain, his despair, his desolation, this loneliness he found so unbearable. I quote Tony verbatim, "I have a cinder block on my chest and I cannot lift or remove it, I find it so hard to breathe." He complained of headaches from pounding that would not stop, the aches of hunger pangs from not eating, and the bouts of vomiting from the knot and pain in his stomach from anxiety, the lethargic feeling from not sleeping. We noticed the deterioration, he had lost 30 pounds in those few weeks from not eating, and this was the visual physical part. What we did not see was the inner turmoil, the quiet emotional breakdown in solitude. I know he tried to spare us the pain he was concealing every time we were near. What we had was a false sense of reparation. We all thought this was a temporary setback and once he got accustomed to the situation, (the failure of his marriage), he would return to his normal self. This never happened.

What was lost? Tony's mental prowess was no longer there. His verbal talents completely vanished into oblivion. We visualized the broken man, who was reverting back to that small child of three, the child who would hide from the crowd because he was shy, the child who would play alone with his toy soldiers and his small matchbox cars for hours on end, the child who became sad when the family had its rough times, through Gina's surgeries, family deaths etc.

What had disappeared? The robust man, the laughing, joking, jovial, successful, bright person we raised so cautiously, so lovingly.

What had remained? The extinguished fire that leaves sooty, gray ashes in a heap too powdery to even hold in the palm of your hands, this was what was left of a person that we nurtured and now we barely recognized.

Still, in all his sadness Tony tried desperately, and obviously succeeded, to convince us all that everything would be okay (maybe deep down he too was hoping that all will be well) or in retrospect was he trying to shadow the real truth from all of us to spare us the pain he was feeling? We will never, ever really know.

When the police officers gathered up all the evidence they found in the car and recorded their findings, they returned the loose album but kept the covers where Tony had scribbled his *good byes.*

Months later as I tried to re-sort my albums, I came across pictures that again gave that dagger in my heart another twist. Most of the pictures were of his wedding day, where everyone was smiling, laughing, kissing etc., all these pictures were precious. The pictures that wrung at my pain reflected the end of the reception where Tony lovingly danced with his **sister**.

To end the perfect wedding celebration, Tony requested the band to play "You've Got a Friend", he invited his sister to dance and then the bride invited her brother to dance. During the dance they exchanged partners. After a while they returned to their original partners but what was really effective and memorable is the four of them interlocked arms and danced as one unit. There was a special wholesomeness and brotherhood (or sisterhood) involved in this maneuver which received such beautiful comments as to the love that was being shared between brother and sister, because in addition to them being family, they were "Friends".

CHAPTER EIGHT

YOU'VE GOT A FRIEND

When you're down and troubled
And you need a helping hand
Nothing, nothing is going right
Close your eyes and think of me
Soon I will be there
To brighten up even your darkness night.

Buddies, pals, comrades, associates, Tony never lacked for any number of friends. He had so many friends and associates throughout his short lifetime that if he would have searched and reached out to any one of them for confidence, help, advice, reassurance, possibly his feeling of isolation would have waned. If he would have just called any one of them to latch on to the thinnest of strings, or grab the life preserver when he felt himself drowning in darkness. If he would have held out his hand, I am sure there would have been many friends who would have shown him there would be a tomorrow and the sun would shine again. Time was all Tony needed. By not reaching out and seeking help, I truly feel Tony did his friends a great disservice. I know he was always there for his friends, because that was Tony, I am certain they would have been there for him.

As I previously mentioned that, as a toddler Tony was selective, more or less, except for Billy Nicholson (who was his shadow) and visa versa. Tony or Billy, either way, they were the "truest of buddies". Tony shared whatever he had. When I asked Billy to comment on their friendship, he remarked "I really cannot say what I feel, or at least I cannot put it into words, just know that Tony is missed very much and it hurts when I think of what we had and what he is missing. Not a day goes by that I don't think of him. Maybe some day I'll get up enough courage to say what is truly in my heart". Billy did relate some funny stories about when they were young men 'out to conquer the world.' A particular episode was when they visited friends in Los Angeles, California, where they entered a 'chest contest', similar to a wet tee shirt contest. Peter, Domenick, Tony and Billy entered the contest and the four of them were winners and they won in that order. They thought they were real he-men but when they reviewed the video tape all they did was *laugh* at such a comical sight.

I stop to wonder at some of these episodes, because looking back when Tony was a young boy he was reserved, somewhat shy and especially very sensitive. In a way I am glad he did at some point break that mold, but then I wonder how far in the opposite direction did he go?. What most of his friends remember is that Tony *needed* to make you laugh.

The shy years were between four and seven. First grade was his 'coming out', when he started performing and gained confidence in himself. Those childhood friends included, Philip DeSarno, Philip's sister Dee Dee short for Diane who between the ages of 9 and 10 was Tony's 'girlfriend', (Tony actually 'stole' a kiss from Dee Dee in the back yard),Anthony Evangelista (Bange) who was also Tony's cousin, Anthony Milandro and Billy Sena to list a few, boy what a group! How fortunate we felt and how blessed Tony was to have shared all these friendships.

There were also Gina's friends that shared Tony's childhood, the closest were Johnny Nicholson, Richard Rizzo, Victor Sena, Alan Shimel, Mario Rizzo, Dana Evangelista, Richard and Elyse D'Angelo . Again, I need not mention how lucky we felt that we had such a conclave of friends for both our children.

This chapter would contain nothing but names if I were to try to include each and every person Tony befriended. There were always the closest ones, then there were the distant ones, the classmates and eventually work associates, even some employers and clients. Some of his adult friends were happy to share some of their recollections, sentiments and comments in eulogy to our precious son. These reflections are from all stages of Tony's life.

As A child:
A Beautiful Message from Maryann Nicholson (Tony recognized as his second mom):

"Now that Tony is gone I often think of those trips he took with us upstate, hiding in the back seat of the car, the swimming pool, the songs and dances, but most of all I remember what a wonderful boy he was. He was always so full of life, so full of fun, so full of love. During his growing up years Tony was such a part of my family that he was like another son. We use to tease him about my daughter Nancy and maybe getting married.

I am so glad that we were a part of his life and that he was such a BIG part of our lives. I believe the saddest day of my life was when I received the phone call saying that Tony had ended his life and then I had to call Billy and Johnny to tell them that their best friend was gone.

Tony will live in our hearts and in our minds forever. The Nicholson family will never forget him. As for now, we will never know or understand what was on his mind that dreadful day for him to take such drastic measures. No one will ever know. When it our turn to go HOME and when we meet again, then and only then, will we know."

As a teenager:
The following letters were received from the Tiseo family who were friends in the truest sense of the word:

From Lina Tiseo:

"We were getting ready to go to church for our nephew's wedding about 2:15 pm on November 29, 1997 and we got a call from Tomassino Varlese. We were told that Tony had passed away. We *wanted to die* , but we had to go ahead with a day that was suppose to be happy and try to celebrate, when inside we were crying in our hearts. We could not hurt our nephew's feelings, but the pain of having to act happy and celebrate will never be forgotten. When we got home that night all we did was cry."

From Pietro Tiseo:

"Dear Jean and Tony, Everyday I pass the cemetery on the Long Island Expressway on my way to work at the airport, I look to my right at the graves and say 'this is where Tony is and sometimes I stop there in my spare time'. The pain is as bad today as it was the day I was told about his passing.

We want you both to know that although there are sad times when we think about the wake and the funeral, these can never override the feelings of happiness and fun memories we had with Tony.

Although the pain you both feel can never be measured; one thing is sure Tony lives in our hearts everyday and will always be remembered as a fun, happy and a very respectful person. His smile, as we mentioned previously, brightened up a room, but surely he will always be remembered for brightening up our lives, each and every one of us. Thank you for giving us the opportunity to put these feelings into words. I guess as time goes on you sometimes forget to realize what an impact Tony made on our lives."

From Tina Conti and Betty Barone (the Tiseo daughters):

"We were at our cousins wedding on November 29, 1997 and we were almost at the end of the wedding when our father came over to us and said 'sit down I have to tell you something that is killing me'. We said 'what happened dad?' The look on his face was so drawn and upset. He told us that Tony Varlese had passed away. Well, we were floored. The rest of the night went by as a big blur. We may not have seen Tony so much at this time, years had caused us to drift apart, but it was a crushing blow."

Domenick and Anthony (the Tiseo sons):

"When we heard about Tony's passing, a few minutes after our sisters did, we were just as upset because Tony was a good friend and will always be our friend.

Tony will live in our hearts forever. May God bless you and your family."

- - * - -

When Tony was floundering from his ups and down in the last few weeks of his life, he inevitably would bring up Steve Gramolini's name as the friend he could confide in and would possibly search for advice and help. Several times, I would respond "I know Steve is your good friend and I know he will be there for you, all you need do is ask." Tony mentioned Steve had an extra bedroom in his home that maybe he would share it with Tony until he got himself together, emotionally. I told Tony this was an excellent idea, he needed to be with someone his own age, someone he would be able to confide in and someone who would understand without casting judgment or recrimination.

Without hesitation Steve was the first friend to share his memories of the friendship he had with Tony.

As an adult -
'A very special friend both to our son and to us' Steve Gramolini wrote:

(Writer's Note: Steve meant these words for me and my husband, but I felt a great need to share them with everyone else. I know Steve won't mind.)

"It is very difficult to relate in words the subtle nuances of a person's voice, the wink of his eye, or a smile. Any of which can mean many things depending on the moment. Tony was a master of expression. Some of the things he said and did will be repeated, mimicked and remembered by his friends forever. It is difficult to experience good times sometimes thinking how much Tony would have appreciated them if he were here. It is not so much a tarnish on those times, but if these times were indeed trophies, well, then they don't shine with as much radiance as they should.

The first time I ever experienced death up close was when my best friend's father passed away; I was about twelve years old. While standing in my neighbor's kitchen after the wake, my neighbor was crying, for he too was a friend of the deceased, his wife came into the kitchen and said 'Why are you crying?' The response was 'I am crying because I am happy'. I immediately understood.

If we believe and have faith in God, and believe that eternal joy and paradise awaits us in heaven with Him, then we should be happy that Tony was the one to get there first."

— - * - —

Along with all Tony's other friends, *I* cannot thank Steve enough for these kind and meaningful words.

When it came to friendship, Andrew (Andy) Daniels (also a co-worker) wishes to remark:

"There was a time when Tony had Spinal Meningitis (1986) and was confined to bed for several weeks and also at that time was studying for the Certified Public Accountant examination. As I recall, that during an audit in Toronto, we had to call him at home to help us with our work. He stayed on the phone with us for hours. He would often challenge other staff members to work as long and hard as he did. Only a few were up to the task. Tony would challenge other accountants' audit findings and would, always with humor, rip their theories to shreds. Thank goodness, I was always on his side. Watching him disprove someone's theory was watching brilliance in the art of debate.

The clients appreciated Tony's knowledge and work ethics so much that they specifically requested that Tony (and ONLY Tony) fly to England on the Concord to help them with the largest real estate construction project since the pyramids. The client's staff loved him."

— - * - —

It was because of this project that Tony and his family got to experience living in London for several months. He thoroughly loved the job, his associates, and especially the country and vowed that some day he would return.

On June 2, 1995 it was to be our 39th Wedding Anniversary and so what do you think Tony came up with as a gift for us? You couldn't even try to speculate. He tried so desperately to do something different, something unique and certainly very elaborate. This time he most definitely outdid himself. We were having dinner at Gina's house one Sunday and he handed us his own computerized version of an anniversary card with an attachment of a First Class, all paid seven day excursion to where else? A trip to London, England. When I say First Class, I mean it was all the way. The airline seats, the stay at the Mayfair International Hotel, Richard Tours to every point of interest one could possibly cram into one week. Even evening excursions which included, the Jack the Ripper streets walk thru, two tickets, front row loge seats at the London Palladium to see "Oliver".

If you think the trip was spectacular, it was. It was not so much the gift that was so monumental; it was that Tony gave of himself. He gave up one week of his own vacation in order to work at his dad's liquor store on Route 25A in Kings Park, so that his dad would be able to take the week off for the trip.

Tony sincerely gave of himself as usual, from the bottom of his heart. As I mentioned over and over again Tony was a giver utmost and foremost. How can one measure this type of love? How can one describe this person who was always so unselfish? Tony's eyes would just light up, like big bright neons, when he saw you were pleased with his gifts. There was always a little twitch of a smile, the smirk, when he made you happy. Happy at the thought that he went out of his way to think of you and give so willingly, so sincerely.

Sometimes I felt that Tony knew I was raised very frugally, simply because I was a depression era child and missed out on a lot of things. As a child, Christmas time always brought me clothes, no toys. Birthdays brought me dinner with family, nothing fun like having a party with friends. My parents experienced difficult times in the 1930's, and were not in a position to allow for luxuries, but somehow a person doesn't miss something they never had. While growing up my home had no radio, no television, no stereo, and so I knew why Tony wanted me to have all those things I lacked as a child.

On the flip side, in raising my children, I made sure they both had those special things which I never had the luxury of having when I was a child growing up.

Josephine La Tempa, a co-worker at Jones, Lang and Wooten and a friend of Tony's, I never had the pleasure of meeting, offered her letter to us in honor of Tony's memory and their friendship:

"I worked with Tony for three years. When I first started, my desk was right outside his office. As time passed, we became good friends. We shared so many family stories. I can recall one morning in his office, for close to an hour, we talked about how our families canned **tomato sauce**. We both got such a kick over the fact that our families still make sauce the same way, with the same type of machine. One day we actually exchanged jars of tomato sauce! He would tell me how he hated onions in his sauce and I would tell him how I loved *extra* onions in my sauce. He would tell me how much he loved his mother's cooking.

I have so many beautiful memories of your son that I keep close to my heart. He was a very good friend to me and I to him. I spoke to him often and always tried to help him and just be there to listen to him. I can never forget him and there is not a day that goes by that I do not think of him.

I want to tell you that on that Wednesday, the day before Thanksgiving the year he died, we spoke and he told me how much he loved his parents and how much closer to you he felt. I hope this letter finds you both well and does not sadden you, that is not my intention. You will always be in my prayers and in my heart, as well as your son. Tony Varlese was a **beautiful person and a wonderful friend** to me. Thank you so much and may God bless you."

-- * --

This mention of Josephine's comment in her letter regarding the tomato sauce, is for those who couldn't possibly imagine that in this day and age there are some families (mostly Italian, I think) who still process food and do their own canning. To say that this is a chore is an understatement. Every Labor Day weekend the Varlese family and their in-laws would spend their time, picking, washing, quartering, boiling, straining, feeding into an automated pulp machine that would separate the skins and seeds from the tomatoes that we would preserve in the sterilized mason jars. The process was exhausting, but the love shared among the family members made the chore so much more enjoyable. At the time when the family was intact we processed about 800 lbs. of tomatoes. This would give the family one year of perfect sauce for the pasta we all consumed.

My husband and I still continue to preserve our tomatoes, but not with the same zest and zeal that was there when the family was intact. The chore now is laborious, boring and a heartache, as I remember the years of fun we had during tomato season. Again, these are the hard times, the joy of family get-togethers, with so much laughter.

I thank Josephine for sharing her tomato stories but most of all for the friendship she offered my son during the good times and the sad times.

As a husband
A letter received from Tony's wife:

When I think of Tony: ***Joking***, all or nothing comes to mind, refusal to fail, loud radio volume and fast reckless driving, love for family, love for sports (those mighty Buffalo Sabres- his favorite hockey team) football (Kansas City Chiefs), baseball (Mets), golf, tennis, Wollyball (a cross between Volleyball and Racquetball), it is easier to try to say what Tony did not like. White chocolate was his favorite candy, Ben & Jerry's Chunky Monkey ice cream, Led Zeppelin, Zebra (a band group he loved to follow when he was a teenager). He loved playing the drums, white water rafting, office softball games, scuba diving, and yes there was Deck Hockey. The games I had to film hours on end in the freezing cold so his team could watch the video and correct their mistakes. One year he won a TROPHY for sustaining the <u>worst injury</u>.

Tony would never waiver on indecision. He knew what he wanted, and usually got it even if he did not think it through. Fall was his favorite season. On Christmas Eve he would still be shopping - the rush is what he lived for during the Holidays.

Cannot forget his traveling, Ohio, Florida, Dallas (Texas), North Carolina, Toronto (Canada), Seattle (Washington), Oregon, California, London (England), traveling on the "Concord", Amsterdam, Paris. There may be other locations I forgot.

He played on some of the most famous golf courses, including Pebble Beach. I know there is a lot more, but it is impossible to remember everything a man like Tony did.

Tony only lived 35 years but he lived life to the fullest of anyone I have ever known even those who lived to be 100 years old. I wonder if he knew somewhere in his soul that he was only going to live to 35. He always seemed to be on the fast track, I always thought that he was running, running , at the time, from me.

After his grandmother died he seemed to get worse. He had stomach problems that required extensive testing (this was tough for Tony, he couldn't even handle giving a urine sample). He began working even longer hours, playing harder too. I don't remember seeing him really grieve his grandmother's death, perhaps he didn't. The morning I last saw Tony he had visited his grandmother's grave. He told me he missed her so much. I should have realized at that point he wanted so desperately to be with her. He told me he wished he knew what she wanted him to do. He told me that no matter what, he would always do what he wanted and no one would or could stop him. The words compromise and patience were a challenge to him.

Tony and his grandmother, what a pair! Tony not only stood by his grandmother, he brought a great amount of laughter into her life. At times "playful" anger too. While working in New York City Tony stayed at his grandmother's house for several months. One particular night he decided to play a joke on his grandmother (one of many). He put a rolled damp washcloth under the sheets toward the foot of the bed. Knowing the exact location to place the washcloth, now he just had to sit and wait.

His grandmother finally decided to go to bed. She climbed into the bed and Tony could barely keep the laughter to himself. The screams came along with the Italian word for "SNAKE". The sheets went flying and he had never seen his grandmother move so fast. When she finally realized that it wasn't a snake but her grandson playing a joke, she grabbed the first thing she could and began hitting him. The love poured out between them that only family could understand. I don't think she talked to him for days but each night after work she had a wonderful Italian dinner waiting for him, along with hand washed and pressed dress shirts. No, I was not in his life at this time but Tony had a special way of telling stories with such emotion (and after I did become a part of his life and getting to know him and his family, I felt as though I was there and could imagine it all).

Tony was driven by his heart and rarely ever thought of the full realm of the consequences of his actions, not calculating the outcome. I have had many dreams of Tony since his death. These dreams have been many guiding dreams, answering questions, helping me make decisions about the boys. I am not sure where I am in understanding the spiritual aspect of all this, but I do believe now that life goes on.

My first dream of Tony was one that was extremely emotional and powerful. He came to me telling me he did not want to be dead. He told me he didn't realize what he was doing or had done. He struggled with accepting death but I believe he has since. There are so many random things that happened in my life and our sons' lives that confirm that he is around.

Both of the boys play in sports and at different seasons received the same numbers on their uniforms that their father had on his uniform when he played. (Keep in mind the boys go to a City school which is fairly large and has many teams. The coaches hand out uniforms randomly based on sizes). The boys were also accepted into teams that were the same as their father or teams that Tony loved.

The most riveting situation that happened while I was planning Tony's funeral, is both eerie and mind boggling. I went into his closet at 11:30 am, I had to pick out the clothes he would be buried in. I fell to the floor and completely lost it once again. I was alone and I started screaming at him "how could you do this, how could you leave your sons if they meant so much to you, how, how, how?"

I wanted time to stand still. I couldn't do this anymore. " I don't have the strength to go on. I can't do this. I want time to stop. Tony you did this final act now you have to carry me through this....."
I laid there crying for a *long* time. I suddenly felt a surge of energy and got up. I looked at my watch, it read 11:32 am. I remember asking myself, "How could be 11:32 am, darn it my watch stopped".

I got up and immediately found what I knew Tony wanted to wear and I came out of the closet. I glanced at the clock on the dresser and it read 12:20 pm. I could not believe it and more importantly when I looked at my watch it began ticking again - it now read 11:35 and kept moving!!! This watch was one of the last gifts Tony had bought me. The band has X's and O's in silver and gold around it with a very simple face. I have never had a problem with the watch since then. I did replace the battery three years later. Even after death, Tony could play a joke, but more importantly I now look back at that energy surge and really wonder.....

The mention of Tony's name

may bring tears to our eyes,

but it never fails to bring

music to our ears.

As his friends, please do not

keep us from hearing

his beautiful music.

You can visit Tony's Website

at

www.tonyvarlesejr.com

CHAPTER NINE

HE AIN'T HEAVY, HE'S MY BROTHER

The road is long with many a winding turn
That leads us to who knows where, who knows when
But I'm strong, strong enough to carry him
He ain't heavy, he's my Brother.

In looking back at one's life, it is difficult to recall your earliest memory. Our capacity to remember is that of being able to retain only the most significant and important events. Time tends to erase many moments that are so real to us in our present everyday life. Memory... I believe this is the one thing that sets humans apart from all other species. But it is the nature of those memories that are different. Yes.... salmon can remember their birthplace, and bees the exact location of a single flower. But humans have a unique system of memory that can be triggered and stimulated. The most powerful of these is the olfactory sense. Smells can bring us back to a time and place we once thought long forgotten. More compelling, is the fact that our emotions can cause us to remember past events, the people, and even places that we once visited.

Whether we truly recall, or just recount, may be one in the same. I clearly remember times that are so vivid, that they seemed to have occurred such a short time ago. The fact may be that the perpetuation of stories or events, through our own recollection or through that of others, is what we perceive as memories.

My relationship with my brother was not extraordinary in the sense that it was in fact as ordinary as any sibling relationship, which in itself is extraordinary. Only now do I realize that.

We can look to the dictionary to define this simple word.
> Brother (brthr)
> n., pl. brothers. Abbs. bro., br., b.
> 1. A male having the same parents as another or one parent in common with another.
> 1. pl. Often brethren (brthrn) One who shares a common ancestry, allegiance, character, or purpose with another or others, especially:
> a. A kinsman, b. A fellow man, c. A fellow member, as of a fraternity, trade union, or panel of judges on a court. d. A close male friend; a comrade. e. A soul brother.

As we all know, these words seem rather flat. One cannot define the meaning of the connection that siblings have.

My earliest memory of Tony was actually not upon our first meeting. It was at the moment I found out about his birth, although what *birth* entailed was a mystery to me back then. As I recall, I was spending the day with my paternal grandparents, affectionately known to me as Grandma Picciarella and Grandpa Raimuccio. It was a comfortable setting to me, as I had spent many hours with them and my cousins who lived just next door to our house on 50th Avenue in Long Island City. I remember the phone ringing, and my Uncle Frank speaking in a loud and happy voice. I vividly recall my grandfather sitting at his usual seat at the head of the dining room table. Grandpa was the one who broke the news that everyone was so happy about. "Gina -

.........you have a baby brother!" I don't know what they expected, but the fact that I did not share in their joy was evident. I responded with disappointment and anger at not getting the sister I hoped for. My response was "Grandpa.. I didn't want a baby brother, I WANT A SISTER!! Tell them to bring him BACK and get me a girl baby."

Grandpa assured me that I would love my baby brother, and I believed him. I knew he would not let me down. After all, it was this very stoic man, who for my third birthday insisted that my parents buy me the Astro Base toy that I had longed for, but was deemed as a "boy's toy" by my mother and father. It was the first of many lessons my parents learned about raising me. It was one of the first incidents of many where I was allowed to dance to that different drummer. Although I did not have the fortune of having very many years with Grandpa Raimuccio, I remember many things about him. His laugh, his voice. The way he always slipped his grandchildren money to go to the nearby candy store. The way he always made sure I was the one who received the birthday cake that remained in the glass that was used to bore out the center of the round cake to make it easier to cut. I vividly remember his partially missing thumb, from an on-the-job mishap, and I somehow identified with his physical impairment.

Tony came into my life when I was just ten days into my fourth year. I was no longer the only child, but I remember being excited at the prospect of having a playmate. Little did I know that this would not occur for a few years. Little did I know that we would have such a few short years.

I can recall certain events, though probably by periodically viewing our 8mm movies so popular in the 1960's. We all can relate to those silent, flickering clips taken by the amateur cameraman many of us called "dad". And who can forget the jumping, waving, and more importantly, squinting subjects as the bank of flood lights hit you right in the eye causing temporary blindness.

One of the funniest of these movies was the Christmas of 1964. We were in our new home in Rosedale, N.Y. I was turning seven and Tony was almost three years old. It was a typical Christmas morning. The tree aglow. Literally! We had one of those new ultra-modern aluminum trees (yes, I said *aluminum*) that was "lit" with a spotlight that had a rotating plastic disc in front of it, the infamous "color wheel". Our tree turned red, then yellow, then blue, and finally green before beginning the cycle all over again. Oh, how Tony **hated** that tree. He would constantly remind me of that "ugly tacky metal" tree we had. Years later, in his own home, he would always **insist** on a real "live" tree. I guess Tony never got over the trauma of having a metal tree.

So there we were, in our small living room, celebrating Christmas in the new house and in front of the newly installed wall of mirrors. Somehow I do not remember any of the gifts I received that year, but what I vividly recall was the gift that Tony received. It was appropriately named "Tony the Pony". This was a motorized version of the typical hobby horse, and very hi-tech for that era. I remember the smell of the plastic, and the huge battery that powered this small ride-on toy. I watched as mom placed Tony on top of his new steed. She instructed my brother how to work the pedals to make it go forward and in reverse. Tony followed mom's instructions, he lurched backward, then in an act of over-reaction, he pressed the pedals full steam ahead into the wall of mirrors. The look of terror and fear was all over Tony's face. He jumped off the robotic stallion, and ran to the other side of the room after crashing headlong into the mirrored wall. It was many weeks before he would attempt to sit upon that horse again.

I find it rather ironic that Tony fell off that horse and *refused* to get back on. My attitude was that I would conquer that horse no matter what it took. That is where my brother and I were so different. I would have loved the challenge, but Tony would not confront those fears until he was ready. I would have broken that bronco, while Tony would wait for it to tame itself. I guess in looking back, Tony really would never set himself up for failure. He really got strength from attempting to do things that he felt were 'safe' and within his realm. He always knew his limitations, and challenged himself within those limits. Sometimes I envied him for having this characteristic. Sometimes I felt sorry for him for being like that. But it was his style, and in retrospect was one of the first indications that Tony wanted all things to be in his control He would challenge them when he was ready, and not before.

There are certain things that we experience, that can only be understood and meaningful to those family members that knew every nuance of our being. It was the day in and day out events that we sometimes remember. Tony and I shared some things that with one short word, would bring us to tears from laughter. How silly they seem years later, but as I write this, I am smiling thinking of some of those funny little verbal triggers. One worders, such as "Boom-Boom". This was our nickname for dad. Dad got this name from us because many times, Tony would sneak into my bedroom at bedtime and we would rough house on the beds, or just get silly and jump around. The telltale sign of when we needed to stop was when we would hear dad coming down the hallway to the bedroom. In his anger, which was mainly because he had to get up from his usual spot on the couch, he would stomp down the hallway. The sound of his steps made us scream "Boom-Boom is coming !" We would immediately quiet down, and pretend that we were just lying on the bed. Of course, Tony would get shuffled back to his room, until the next night, then the ritual began all over again. We had so much fun on those nights. We would imitate, over and over again, the things we found funny. Like the "Puffa Puffa Rice" song or the "Happy Anniversary" song from one of our favorite episodes of the Flintstones. We always went to sleep tired from laughing so much, and always with a smile on our faces.

When I was younger, I had the normal sibling jealousy that all kids experience. I now had to share my time with mom and dad. Leave it to me to figure out how to use this little brother to my advantage. He became my unknowing scapegoat. I finally had someone else to blame things on! I thought I had all this down to a science, but being a parent myself, I now know that it is almost impossible for a six year old to command a credulous story especially when you were trying to save your own skin. I can say that I clearly remember constantly being in trouble. I was always curious and daring, so naturally things would get dirty, or broken and even lost.

So now there it was, a very large Diffenbachia plant. It was a large specimen that just sat in our living room, next to the couch. This plant was my nemesis and the source of a few incidents for me. The first incident involved this freshly watered plant being knocked over, rather forcefully, by me. I knew I was going to be in big trouble, so I quickly thought to hide all the mud that fell on the light beige living room rug. My mother had very conveniently placed a small throw rug under the plant so as to protect the new wall-to-wall carpeting. I quickly swept all the mud into one pile, and then covered it with the throw rug, and topped it off with the plant. "There!" I thought, "out of sight, out of mind". I cannot recall all the details, but it did not take long for mom to discover my secret. Oh, that plant!

The second time I encountered trouble with this very same plant was the time my father had a discussion with me regarding the toxicity of this Diffenbachia species. He told me that the plant would actually cause someone to lose their voice if chewed. I guess I was always scientifically inclined, even at the age of six. I needed to actually prove to myself that this plant held such magical powers. I proceeded to make exacting bite marks around the edges of some of the large glossy green and white leaves. When my parents discovered these marks, I immediately blamed it on Tony. What I had not taken into account was that Tony was only two years old at the time, and had far few teeth than I had at six. Positive forensic identification was easily and quickly made, and I once again paid the consequences. I am not sure how long that plant lived with us, but I do remember trying to stay as far away from it as I could.

As Tony and I grew older, he came to trust me to do certain things for him. I had always had a knack for cutting hair, and that was probably due to all the "practice" I had in giving all my dolls haircuts. I must say that by the time I gave my brother a haircut, I had sufficiently mutilated many a Barbie doll.

One summer evening, on the deck in our backyard in Kings Park, I grabbed a comb and a pair of scissors and sat my brother down. He was about twelve years old at that time. In attendance was my maternal grandparents, as they were going to be watching us later in the evening, while my parents went out. I clearly remember my grandfather sitting near me watching as I tried to cut Tony's hair while he squirmed around in the seat. My grandmother kept yelling at him to stay still. As I was putting the final touches to the haircut trying to make sure it was trimmed evenly on his sideburns, Tony jerked his head to the side, just as the blades of the scissors closed around the tip of his earlobe. He immediately clasped his hand to his ear and cried "Aye-aye-yah!!!!" I protested loudly and quickly blamed him for not having heeded my warning not to move, and was rather shocked to see his hand covered in blood, after he quieted down. The only sound that remained was my grandfather's distinctive hissing laugh, as he could not believe that I had snipped a bit of Tony's earlobe right off. Needless to say my mother was more angry at her parents for finding Tony's pain a source of humor. We recounted this haircut incident for many years thereafter and only then did we also find some humor in the scenario.

From previous chapters you may have surmised that Tony was a very accident prone child. For someone who was basically timid and cautious, he had more than his share of bumps, bruises and stitches.

He also had a very weak stomach when it came to sighting blood, as evidenced by his cringing every time you even mentioned his scar from his appendectomy, his scar from falling in the backyard, etc. In an emergency he would seek me out if I was in the area, I even had priority over my mother, as she too had a real weakness in times of any emergency especially anything involving blood. I somehow became Tony's protector, his nurse, his physician.

I recall one particular event, on a hot summer afternoon when I was about seventeen and Tony was fourteen. On this day, we were enjoying our backyard pool, with our Kings Park friends having joined us. Mom and dad had to attend a party, so I was left in charge. Tony had two friends over and I also had two friends there. Eventually, the frolicking in the pool evolved into a playful water fight. I watched from a lounge chair while Tony and his friends gathered buckets of water and began dousing each other. They took turns running around the pool trying to evade each others' stream of water. In his hurry to avoid an approaching bucket, Tony ran toward the side of the house and slipped on the newly installed brick walkway. Unfortunately his ankle grazed the sharp edge of one of the bricks and ended up with a deep laceration on his foot, near his ankle. I took one look at his injury and knew we needed to get him to a hospital quickly. I dispatched my friends to the neighbors, and everyone ran in different directions to find an adult that could assist. As they were scurrying I moved Tony to the front lawn. The first neighbor to arrive was the man directly across the street from our house. He offered to take Tony to the nearest hospital, St. John's Episcopal in Smithtown. I decided to stay behind and try to get in touch with my parents. The neighbor placed Tony in the car and one of his friends rode with them. I ran to the phone to get a message to my parents. In the following frantic minutes, I recall a rather comic scene unfolding in front of our house. With all of our friends scattering to get assistance, my good friend Eydie Palmieri and her brother ran home, a few houses down from ours, to get help. As I waited on the front porch for any news from the neighbor who drove Tony to the hospital, I saw my girlfriend's large German Shepherd running up the block towards me. Behind the dog was my girlfriend and her siblings, and pulling up the rear was her grandfather driving *five miles an hour in his Jaguar*. They were coming to help, but the dog would have probably made it to the hospital faster!

Needless to say, because I was still considered a minor, the hospital refused to treat Tony without consent from my parents. I recall arguing with the nurse from the emergency room who had called me for information. She assured me that Tony was okay, and was not going to bleed to death in the interim. My parents arrived at the hospital shortly thereafter only to find a scared, frightened and shivering son. In all our haste, Tony and his friend went to the hospital wearing only their wet bathing suits. Tony received many stitches and a new sense of the admonition by our parents when told "stop running, or you will hurt yourself".

Lessons learned, debts paid. Life moves slowly on.

Somehow, through the years we learn the importance of things only after they are gone. For those of us that are left behind, we realize all too late the words we never said, the hugs we neglected to share, the times we took for granted are things we can never retrieve. How can we repay those debts to our guilt other than to replace them with the thoughts and memories of the times we did use the opportunity to share those very same things. Life holds many surprises for all of us. We can only hope that they will be happy. We can only hope that one day, the happiest surprise is that all of us will be together, living in a world that will never have an end....

OUR SEASONS

The Summer sun does shine, but we don't care,
There is no joy for us to share.
The cold will come, but not too soon,
For us to hide in Winter's gloom.

At last the leaves begin to fall,
Stoic trees so stark and tall.
The gray of night we won't dread,
With every leaf a tear is shed.

With all these tears, the snow we melt,
Like prism ice is how we felt.
Sadness stays within our hearts,
The drama unfolds, we play our parts.

The buds and blooms show their face,
With rainbow hues in awe and grace.
Not for us my child so dear,
Shades of blue is what we fear.

Warmth of sun and bright are days,
With springtime here in many ways.
Thawing chill shall fade inside,
Our love for you shall not subside.

Tony's lilacs are almost here,
A flower that he loved so dear.
Near his stone so carefully placed,
Reminding us of his smiling face.

Easter church bells loudly chime,
This was Tony's favorite time.
To wait and hear the robins sing,
We pray our Lord, return our Spring.
Mom and Dad

CHAPTER TEN

MEMORY

Memory, all alone in the moonlight
I can smile at the old days
I was beautiful then
I remember the time I knew what happiness was
Let the memory live again

Memories are sometimes sweet, hopefully seldom they are bitter, mainly they are happy, some are regrettable, and then there are those that are sad. Memories can create emotions all intertwined, woven together and then raveled into one substance when someone is trying to capture something that has been lost. This is all we have left of our son, our memories and those memories he created with a multitude of friends. Are these memories enough for us to hold on to and try to continue living? Only time will tell.

Our morning prayer begins and our evening prayer culminates with Tony's name. Every day ends very much the same way, whispered in soft sobs grasping the celebration of our son. Our testimonial is beyond beautiful because Tony was beautiful, not solely in the physical sense of the word, for he was a beautiful child of God. Tony's beauty was his spirit, his inner personality which was pure and honest and that his soul belonged to God, so how could he not be beautiful.

In the stories, the episodes, the escapades, the outings, the sharing of time with Tony, the encounters, the business and personal contacts, you can readily read and spy immediately that Tony's personality was that of a very sincere, caring and most of all a loving person. Each and every narrative, each chronicle, whether it be from family or friends, communicates the kindness he had and the goodness he shared with everyone. He imparted his amiability with true feeling. He was neither a superficial nor an artificial person. There was no pretense in his friendships, no hidden agenda, just sincerity in its truest form. Sometimes, because of all these memories and tributes, the sadness is even more overwhelming and very difficult to accept that Tony's presence here is now only spiritual.

A beautiful memoir from Cousin Frank Varlese Jr.

Frankie Varlese was not one of Tony's buddies; he was his first cousin. He was eight years older than Tony so the childhood memories are different. Frankie thought of Tony as the tag-along-kid. Of the three cousins Diana was the oldest by two years senior to Frankie who was the middle child and Rosemary was the youngest, she was three months younger than Gina. The four of them, Diana, Frankie, Gina and Rosemary were the team leaders, and Tony being the youngest just followed whatever the gang was doing. There certainly were many times they all got into trouble as a team. I remember one particular Sunday afternoon. We all had dinner at Grandma Varlese's house and had just finished eating so my sister-in-law Mary and I were helping our mother-in-law with the dishes. The children went upstairs to Mary's apartment to play. We heard them scurrying from one room to the next, their laughter was loud and plentiful. When the running back and forth became exceptionally boisterous, Mary and I ascended the stairs to check on these *playful* children. I think Tony was not quite three years old at that time so he certainly was somewhat innocent of the mischief that was occurring.

Diana and Frankie had a lime green, yellow breasted pet parakeet at that time, whose name was Petey. That day no one " fessed" up to who let Petey out of the cage, but when they heard us climbing the stairs it was Frankie who caught Petey and put him under his cardigan sweater and into his armpit to hide the fact that Petey was out of the cage. In his haste to hide the poor doomed parakeet, he didn't realize how forceful he had been or how fragile the parakeet was, and so Petey's neck snapped and died in the midst of their laughter. The laughter quickly halted when the damage was realized and then the reality of the seriousness of their playing had ended in sadness and the tears started flowing from all of them. We are not sure if the tears were solely for Petey or the fact that they knew they were in deep trouble.

This was an episode Frankie recalls very vividly, but what he recalls most about his cousin is that Tony was such a genuine good person, as a child and certainly as an adult.

A Note from a Dear Cousin- Frankie's sentiments about the adult Tony:

"Some mornings I wake up and for just a moment I feel that Tony is still with us here on earth and expect him to be present at the next family gathering. It is then that I realize that he is gone and left us too soon, never to be seen in this lifetime again. To say it is sad is an understatement.

I still try, to this day, to understand what led this gentle person to make the ultimate decision to end his life. He had a great career, two beautiful children and was well liked and respected by everyone he met. He was easy to talk to and had a unique sense of humor. In all the years I knew Tony, he never once had a disparaging remark or negative comment to make about anyone. He certainly could make you laugh without having someone as the target of his humor. He loved his family, all of them including us and was loved by all of us in return.

I have always felt the need to ponder over and try to explain why tragedies happened in my life. These explanations help give me a sense of relief and try to find hope.

I see now, Tony was a man of deep sensitivity and had great integrity. He needed to blame himself for his failing marriage. He had convinced himself that he alone was responsible for his marital problems. He had convinced himself that it was solely his fault for everything that was wrong and mainly that he had "let his children down", how untrue. Tony's only sin was that he worked long hard hours to support his family and try to give them the best that life had to offer.

In his final days, Tony could not bear the pain of his 'self inflicted guilt' and what he spoke of as feeling betrayed by the one person he loved the most. I am sure he felt such an unbearable isolation and arrived at his own solution to end this terrible pain he was experiencing.

From time to time, mainly in the morning hours, I find myself thinking of Tony. It is then I begin to pray for him and the rest of the family. My prayers are for the peace and serenity that only God can grant to each and everyone of us.

Dear Aunt Jean and Uncle Tony you have all my love and support forever."

Frank Raymond Varlese

- - * - -

We cannot thank Frankie enough for expressing his feelings and capturing Tony's inner feelings. We feel fortunate that Tony will be remembered with such beautiful thoughts and understanding and that Frankie continues to respect Tony's memory. I received other memoirs that reflected Tony, capturing his thoughts and gestures throughout his short life. Each one is a tribute, a monument of sadness, but most of all reciprocal love shared while in life and now in death.

A close co-worker from Clarion Partners wrote:
"I am a friend of Tony's and his death is still so difficult to comprehend. Several years of working together, we became close, especially the last two years of his life. I often contemplate our last conversations and wonder what I might have missed that could have changed what he did to himself and to us. Till this day, I still question myself as to why I never called to check on him that Thanksgiving Day, maybe it would have changed something, maybe I would have said some words that would make him reconsider. I did not call because I was struggling with the first anniversary of my father's death, and it was a bad time for me, but I never realized how much worse it would get when I heard the news about my dear friend and sushi partner Tony. I have so much to share and my heart is still so heavy. You have left a wonderful tribute to your son and I am sure if he never knew before, he certainly is aware now how much his parents and so many others love him."

From Cousin Rosemary Varlese Killikelly:
"As the tears of disbelief swell up in my eyes, I try to think of some happier and funnier times. I recall the time Tony, Gina, Frank and I went to Carvel. I remember Tony had a vanilla shake (or a banana barge?) I'm not sure. What is vivid is Tony was eating this ice cream concoction as big as his head. He kept repeating, 'I caught a really big fish!'. He shoveled a gigantic spoonful of ice cream into his mouth. Uncle Tony warned him to take it easy. We all laughed at Tony's silliness, and the warning was no match to the fun of the moment. Yes, it was bound to happen, Tony turned a white shade of pale and the back door of the black station wagon was wrenched open in split second timing. It was a sight that we recounted for many years as the night Tony had to let go of 'all those fish'."

Tony's close friend John Nicolette fondly remembers:
"I'm not exactly sure where or when it was that I first met Tony. It was sometime around 1980 or 1981. We were going to college together at C.W. Post and working together at Pathmark in Commack. In addition, we spent what must have been all of our spare time 'hanging out'. During this period we became the best

of friends. It seemed we did everything together. From ball games, to concerts, to vacations, to card games. We had a million laughs together. To me, this was one of ***Tony's greatest gifts, the ability to make people laugh.*** Whenever I was going to be seeing Tony, I knew it wouldn't be long until I was going to be laughing hysterically.

Tony got an accounting job soon after graduation. I eventually got a job at a Wall Street brokerage. Due to our new found responsibilities and obligations we didn't see each other quite as often, but we tried to get together whenever possible. In 1987 I moved to Tokyo. As one could imagine, with such a great distance between friends and seeing each other so infrequently, it was inevitable that the closeness we shared would wane. Gradually, I lost touch with all my high school and college friends with the exception of Tony and Steve Gramolini. I visited the United States twice a year and made it a point that I'd get together with Tony and Steve at least once for a big night out. This usually consisted of a huge steak dinner at one of Manhattan's finest, followed by a card game that lasted into the wee hours of the morning. Even though we saw each other only twice a year now, when we did get together it was as if we had seen each other just yesterday. Nothing was different.

Tony was his usual witty, humorous self, keeping us in stitches all evening. However, we weren't a part of each other's daily lives. I was not aware of any problems Tony was having and cannot help wonder if he might have reached out to me had I been living back home in the states.

The way I'll remember Tony most was the last time I saw him. It was during one of my visits to the states. We tried and tried to make the usual plans I just mentioned, but Tony was just too busy and wasn't going to be able to find the time to get together, no matter how much Steve and I busted his chops to try to make it. So, Steve and I went to The Palm anyway regretting the fact that Tony wasn't with us. The day before I was to return back to Tokyo, which was usually a somber day around the house knowing we wouldn't be seeing each other for another six months or so, my mom fixed a tray of veal cutlet parmigiana and a tray of chicken cutlet parmigiana as a last day send-off meal. While I was standing in the kitchen, I noticed a car pull up in front of the house and out popped Tony. His unannounced visit was a complete surprise, since he had made it very clear that he was very busy. Needless to say, we had a great evening. Tony had dinner with my family and me. When I asked Tony what he preferred, chicken or veal, he gave his patented teeth gritting response, "WHADDA YOU THINK?" Veal it was. We enjoyed a few beers and wine while Tony kept me and my family entertained for hours. I can still see his face, lit up with enthusiasm, as he delivered one laugh filled story after another.

I don't know if Tony's brand of humor was appealing to everyone, but he certainly provided me with tons of laughter and many fond memories. I often think of the many things we enjoyed together and consider myself lucky to have known him. The sad part is there won't be any new ones."

Addendum: "Mrs. Varlese, I'm sure you are well aware that I have SO MANY memories of the times I spent with Tony. I think of him often and those times we spent together. I have recollections of experiences that just the two of us shared, that we use to enjoy talking about together, that I can't share with him anymore. *It saddens me that it had to be this way.*"

Next is one of many episodes and memories that Steve Gramolini, a special friend, was gracious enough to share with us:

MY TAXES

"One of the episodes that always makes me laugh was a time when Tony came over to do my taxes. Tony would never accept any money from me, so in lieu of payment, we would always go out for a nice dinner somewhere and I would pick up the tab.

As you know, we always prided ourselves on our cooking prowess. Hence, this tradition was founded at the JETS football games that we would never allow hamburgers or hot dogs on the grill. (Not that there is anything demeaning about hamburgers or hot dogs). It was just that **gourmet** was our way. Therefore, anytime we went out for a meal, you can rest assured that the restaurant we chose was of the highest quality.

Tony came out to Long Beach on a snowy night in March. We really did not want to drive too far in bad weather so we tried to find a place nearby. A new seafood restaurant had opened on Long Beach Road a few months prior and had received good reviews in the local paper, as well as from some friends of mine who had already dined there. We figured, 'Great! Let's go have a feast on some lobster, shrimp, crab meat cocktail, etc.' We could not believe our amazing good luck. Tony was already exclaiming in his usual 'Aaaah! Let's take my car Rub (a nickname he had for me, whence it came from I can't recall), we'll never get there in that piece of scrap metal you drive'. So we grabbed a couple of Heinekens and jumped into his white Mercury Cougar. We are now driving on Long Beach Rd., and we see the restaurant coming up on the right hand side of the road, so we slow down to pull into the parking lot while trying to crane our necks to make sure the place looked open. We cruise into the lot and stop near the restaurant entrance so that we could look inside through these huge windows with those white crisscross patterned grills. We must have taken about five seconds to take in the oak and galley like atmosphere that one would find in many fine seafood restaurants. Before that view could sink in and whet our appetites, we both spied, at the same time, the one thing that changed everything. It is actually closer to being an American icon. Oscar Madison cherished it and once referred to it as tomato wine. It is probably one of the closest things to perfection that man has ever mastered besides Coca-Cola and ninety feet between bases on the diamond. When going out for a fine gourmet meal, however, there are certain things that one does not expect to see on the table when peering through a window. One might expect nice linen on the table, a small lamp and perhaps a candle, an arrangement of flowers, maybe even a decorative place setting. Tony spied exactly what I saw at the same time and turned to me. We both looked at each other and simultaneously shouted 'KETCHUP ON THE TABLE!' Tony pedaled his foot on the gas, did a 180 degree turn, skidding through the snow, sped onto Long Beach Rd., and we drove until we found a place that we deemed worthy. There are just some things in this world we just didn't settle for."

- - *- -

In their defense, I guess maybe I may have had something to do with Tony's culinary idiosyncrasies. There are the recollections, which still today makes me very melancholy. During the Summer of 1995, Tony was really getting into his Saturday morning golf outings with the Jones, Lang and Wooten team of co-workers and friends. He would, without a whimper, get up at the ungodly hour of five o'clock in the morning to meet with his golf partners and get an early tee-off. When he would finish the game, which was usually about twelve noon, he would stop by directly at our house for lunch. Without hesitation, I would always make him whatever favorite notion or craving he had for that particular day, especially my preserved pickled eggplants, which went well with cold cut sandwiches. Prosciutto was his favorite cold cut, as I previously mentioned, and knowing that he would show up on Saturdays, I would try to have his favorite luncheon for him.

What was more memorable was the fact that we would, after lunch, plan our dinner menu for that evening. Tony and I would go through my gourmet cookbooks, of which I had quite a few, and look for something exotic, different, of course it always turned out complicated and very involved. We would then make a shopping list and his dad would go to Key Food to purchase whatever we didn't have in the pantry.

Tony would then call his wife with excitement and asked that she pack up the kids and come over to our house for dinner, which he and I would gladly and proudly prepare. It was fun in selecting the right meal, gathering up the ingredients, washing, chopping, mincing, dicing and cooking etc. At that time we still owned the Liquor Store on Rte.25A in Kings Park and, of course, the wine selection was for the taking. From our wine tasting experiences, we had to select the appropriate wine to compliment the selected meal. Tony's favorite meat was veal, so osso bucco or veal birds, including veal scallopini, veal marsala were always available. Without the need to elaborate we always succeeded to prepare and execute this perfect meal, with the proper settings, the fancy china dinnerware, the Sunday silverware, the brocade linens and napkins and the crystal stemware.

It was not in the cooking and eating that we obtained the greatest joy, though this didn't hinder it; it was the togetherness, the loving atmosphere, the laughs, the happiness that we all shared. It is this closeness that is greatly missed, it is this sharing that presents a void, it is this love that has gone out of my life and created an emptiness that can never, never be filled.

Tony developed culinary skills simply because he had a gourmet palate and loved to eat. He really enjoyed his food as part of his enjoyment of life itself. Though he relished (no pun intended) in priding himself in being able to select good food, in consuming a great meal, dining in elegance, but he also was just as happy at home and in a backyard atmosphere of American hot dogs and hamburgers. It was his capacity of encompassing the full extent of his senses, sight in seeing friends, family in togetherness, tastes of plain or exotic fares, hearing the sound of laughter accompanying the in tandem union of his company, the feeling of just being alive and well, that brought the most joy to his heart.

One evening, January 8, 1993 he took it upon himself to take the day off from work so he could go grocery shopping, come home and cook a **great** meal, by himself, for his wife's birthday. He diligently shopped for the food, carefully selected the appropriate wine, and made sure his wife was away for a few hours and proceeded to wreak havoc in the tidy, neat kitchen at 27 Eugene

Drive.   I remember him using every pot available,   dishes were
strewn everywhere, a chaotic situation was certainly underfoot.
But again, it was his avidity that brought the evening to its
culminating triumph.   I am not sure how his wife interpreted
Tony's zest because it took hours to reassemble the kitchen back
to its original state of tidiness.   Tony had invited his dad and me
to this festive night and yes I did help with some of the
preparation and the cleaning up but what I remember most is
how much love went into that day.   After the meal, the cake, the
singing, the gift giving, we sat for hours nursing a bottle or two of
Amarone.   This wine was one of Tony's favorites together with
Ruffino Classico Reserve.   The warmth that abounded that
evening came from Tony's heart not from the vintage.   It was the
grape that might have had the effect of laughter, but it was his
love that was entrenched to us all that had the astounding effect
of happiness one could never forget.

Our son always had a knack for attempting the unusual, outdoing
himself, go the one step beyond, doing it his way, sometimes to a
point of exasperation.   There were times when his mind was
made up on how to do something and there was no changing it.
There were times he was stubborn to a fault.   If he wanted to buy
something, if he wanted to eat something, if he wanted to go
somewhere, if he wanted to do nothing at all, and of course, if
you tried to convince him otherwise there was no argument.   We
thank God this trait of his was seldom median, this negativity of
his seemed to exacerbate itself when he was extremely tired and
overworked.   Nonetheless at times it did exist, but his 180 degree
turn would erase whatever the opposition was at the time and he
would return to his benevolent self.   The normal Tony, the happy
Tony, would return to us quickly.

Here is an episode that Steve Gramolini shared with us regarding
one of Tony's turn at cooking and eventually a spontaneous
outburst that is still remembered by him and John Nicolette,
remembered as a humorous event by all in attendance.

THE TAILGATE PARTY

"One time we were on our way to the JETS game at the Meadowlands and it was Tony's turn to cook and, therefore, his turn to drive. Tony brought the usual specialties from the Varlese household. That day's menu consisted of veal rollatini, garlic bread and pasta on the side. When it came to the tailgate parties, Tony and I were usually the most creative. It did however, put us under pressure and made getting TO the game that much more of a priority.

We were able to get over the Whitestone Bridge without any problems. This completion of the first leg of the journey was usually inaugurated by the opening of a cold beer for everyone. (Sorry folks, but we were not as concerned or conscience of the dangers of drinking and driving back then). Anyway, we got into traffic as soon as we got to the Cross Bronx and Tony was having a canary fit. He was particularly annoyed at a woman who was blocking his opportunity to pass. She had this look of bewilderment on her face and wasn't really paying attention to what she was doing. This irritated Tony, so he started spewing a stream of obscenities at her while making several theatrical gestures with both his hands (the Italian in him). After finally passing her, he downed his beer in celebration of his passing victory and yelled back at John (Nicolette), who happened to be sitting next to the cooler, 'Get me another beer!' to which John responded indignantly, 'What? Reach back here and get it yourself!' Tony then replied with his usual sneer, **I thought I put you in charge of getting me my beer!'** We were in total hysterics over this comeback. We laughed so hard that we were practically bouncing off the windows for five minutes. My brother Mike could hardly breathe and Tony was barely able to drive straight. It was a perfect comeback, a show-stopper, and a heart punch aimed right at the inconsiderate back-seat passenger. When we finally calmed down, John attempted some feeble comeback line that Tony was all over John before he could even finish his sentence. 'WHY DO I HAVE TO REMIND YOU THAT YOU ARE THE LAMB AND I AM THE SHEPHERD'.

This was just too too much; we were still reeling from the first beer line. We laughed ten times harder than the first time, to the point that we were all in tears. We could not carry on a conversation after that. Any time you were able to catch your breath, you got out one good sign and then went hysterical again. It became contagious. This went on until we arrived at the stadium parking lot.

I can't remember who we were playing or whether or not the JETS won, but I will never forget that drive to the stadium, or what we all consider to be some of Tony's greatest lines."

- - * - -

As a mother I could yell at him one minute and kiss him the next. I understood him without a doubt. I knew he was kind and loving and his outbursts meant absolutely nothing. What I didn't understand was his reluctance to fight when the end was near, his giving up on the one thing he cared for the most, his loss of will power when it was the most crucial, his non-acceptance of what seemed to be a failure, his harboring of guilt for himself for which he had no cause, his severing himself from the one who truly loved him the most, myself. Oh! How I love this son of mine. He was my life.

Roberta and Joe Bublé, Tony's co-workers and friends, could not remember Tony having culinary talents, maybe it was well before he had decided it was fun eating gourmet food and so he had better develop a knack for cooking.

Robert and Joe Bublé in testimony of Tony's cooking skills, Roberta remembers:

"Tony was never the 'cook' of the group, but whenever we traveled with him to Nags Head or the chalet in the Catskills, he would always volunteer and attempted to scramble *burnt* eggs, but in the summer we must confess, Tony made a mean fruit salad. He would cut and display his fruit so precisely. It must have been the accountant in him. Then he would always have to show it off. He would be so proud of himself. For those who don't believe Tony had any cooking abilities, I have pictures to prove it.

Tony was a big part of our lives. We had a chance to grow together and share in many special times. We were honored to have him take part in our wedding day, as we were honored to take part in his. We were fortunate to get to know his family and he got to know ours. We will always remember him and hold him close in our hearts. May God bless you Tony. We miss you very much."

Roberta and Joe

-- * --

Throughout this entire biography, I always make reference to Tony being my life. I have written this and I have constantly verbalized this comment. In retort I would always hear the sympathetic statement 'you have your daughter and her children still. Aren't they part of your life? Don't they fill that void?' Yes, they certainly do and if it weren't for them, I would not be as sane as I am. I am positive I would have been institutionalized by this time. They are my salvation, they are my strength, they are my somewhat willingness to continue to live. Do I present a burden to them? You bet. I am not and never will be the person I was before my son left this world. This does not mean I love my daughter and her family any less, it means I do not have the intact family I once had. An appendage is missing from my body; does it mean the rest of my body doesn't function? No, but it functions laboriously. The everyday routines are fatiguing. Some days getting out of bed becomes strenuous, challenging and I find myself struggling to cope with mundane chores. There is this constant enigma surrounding my everyday existence.

Receiving and reading the escapades that Tony shared with his friends brought smiles to my face, tears to my eyes, but an enormous amount of joy to my heart. It is in keeping memories alive in my mind and heart that allows me to persevere; it enables me to endure these tortuous moments of sadness.

Here is another of Steve's memorable recollections:

WHERE ARE THE KEYS?

"We were at a JETS game again, many of the usual suspects were present. It was a typical New Jersey Meadowlands swamp like day. Cloudy, gray, with a constant rain and mist. The JETS played the most boring game in the world and lost 9 to 3 or something close to that, to some terrible team. The Falcons? Anyway, after the game we decided to play some footfall while we waited for the traffic to dissipate. Midway through our game it started to rain harder so Tony ran over and threw all our jackets into the back of John Nicolette's car. We finished the game about a half-hour later, and ran for the last beer and the warmth of a dry car. Guess what? We were locked out.

John's keys were locked inside the car and the second set of keys, with the can opener, was in the pocket of Tony's jacket on the back seat of the locked car. Why Tony decided to lock the doors behind him when we were playing only a few feet away was a mystery and a subject we harped on for a long time. After a long debate, we couldn't figure out who the bigger idiot was, John or Tony, so we tried to break into the car. We were able to get into the trunk of the car because it didn't have a lock. We proceeded to try to take apart the heavily bolted down back seat so we might be able to get at the keys in Tony's jacket. We were doing this for at least a half hour when we finally decided we should go for help. One of the guys ran back to the stadium and found the security booth where they immediately dispatched a courtesy Meadowlands emergency tow truck. We couldn't believe it when he showed up about five minutes later. He tried to snake his way through the window but to no avail. Now he went for his toolbox, removed a hammer and screwdriver and broke the door lock in one shot. We were so grateful that we tipped him and left him the six pack of imported beer on the passenger seat side of his truck. He thanked us, shut the truck door and we in turn thanked him again. We all shook hands and made a mad dash into John's car. John turned the key in the ignition and started the car and we were just about ready to take off and leave when the guy from the tow truck began banging on the driver's window. He had locked *himself* out of his truck and his truck was running!!! He told us where his station was and asked that we stop there to get one of his buddies to bring him an extra set of truck keys. Before we got to the station, we debated whether we should just blow him off and leave him there awhile. We figured sooner or later someone would miss him and they would go get him. We were really anxious to get on our way and return home. Reality set in and we quickly, without hesitation, wrote off that idea because he WAS pretty cool and he DID save our sorry butts. Besides, we figured God would surely punish us for such an act of indifference. We did the right thing, we went for help and drove home exhausted, conjuring up the events of this miserable day, but we continued to laugh when we recollected the irony of the whole night."

- - *- -

These were a few of those happier times, the joyous ones where these wholesome young men had fun, enjoyed each other's company, stood by each other and were very moral at the right time and at the right situation.

John Nicolette, Tony's other close friend, gave his beautiful rendition of his friendship with my son, but I do recall and I know John won't mind my narrating my version of what happened one Friday evening at my home when the two of them, as teenagers, were just crashing out.

At our Kings Park home we had a beautiful finished basement, with an extra kitchen, a living room, and a drum room where Tony would sometimes harbor himself , shut the door and beat on the drums till all hours of the night. We had a room with a regulation size pool table, television, stereo, etc., certainly the comforts for recreational activities for all their friends. This particular night when John and Tony had nowhere to go, they decided to beat the drums, play pool and finish off a couple of six packs. This was okay with us because our rule was never drink and drive. After they felt they had enough they would just go off into a sound sleep and when they woke up in the morning, I would have the pancakes ready for them. John would always phone his parents to let them know he intended to sleep over. All bases were covered; they were in good hands.

My husband and I retired at our normal bedtime hour and left the bedroom door open so we would be able to hear the music and the goings-on in the basement. I often slept with one eye open, and always both ears to the ground. There wasn't anything abnormal or anything too unusual that I had to fret about. There were just the two of them, not a whole crowd, how much trouble could they get into. Well, I was wrong.

It seems, behind the couch in the drum room, there was a broken heavy-glassed 12" flower vase standing up with the jagged pieces facing upward. I had no idea when it got broken and no idea that it was even there. Lo and behold, after having a few beers the two of them started wrestling, jousting, and laughing at a very loud pitch. Then Tony accidentally fell off the couch and landed smack on his back onto the protruding glass, which was pointed straight up. This was not the strange part of the catastrophe. From the version of the story I was told it took five minutes to determine which one of them was injured. They had stopped horsing around when they spotted blood splattered all over the wall, all over the couch and all over the floor. They sobered up within two seconds. The two of them quietly climbed the stairs to our bedroom, and Tony gently whispered through the door "I think I have a hole in my back." Yes, there was a hole in Tony's back about 1-1/2" wide and 3/4" deep. He was holding a large bath towel over the hole plugging up this gap in his back.

I am not sure where I gathered up enough strength to get out of bed, dress as quickly as I could and then be able to drive to St. John's Hospital at 2:00 am. Because of the enormous amount of blood still gushing from his back, he was seen in the emergency room *immediately*. Of course, he required sutures both inside and outside. I still don't know what kept me together that night. Luckily I did accompany Tony, with John in tow, to the hospital because the attending physician thought perhaps he had been in a bar fight and someone had stabbed him. I reassured him this was not the case. Do you really think if Tony had been in an altercation he would have stopped to telephone his mother, had this been the scenario the hospital personnel envisioned?

Reflecting back, it was a fortunate situation that I kept myself composed, but more fortunate that Tony came through as well as he did that evening. The wound was so deep the glass missed his lungs by a small fraction.

On our way home from the hospital, even with such a serious possibility, Tony and John found something very amusing about the evening's mishap. It seems, when they spotted the blood, neither one of them knew where it had come from. They were not sure who had been injured. They had been having a grand old time and an accident in his own home, such as this, was so unbelievable and so we laughed at the irony that it was I who said that I preferred them to stay home where I could keep an eye on them and know that they were **safe**. Boy! was I ever mistaken. If you are keeping score, this was Tony's 4th E.R. escapade.

Even with the sad stories, I am still grateful that Tony shared such precious times with his friends. Tony's home and heart were always open to all his friends. I loved seeing them and I loved receiving their memories of the good happy times as well as the questionable sad ones.

A Recollection from Andy Daniels of their friendship:

"Our friendship grew around our humor, our interests and appreciation of each other's athletic abilities and our work ethics.

I personally found Tony to be much like myself. He was a class clown, yet had a warm side that I know some did not see. I was lucky to have known both sides of Tony. We often spoke of real issues of life, dating, sex, marriage, careers and family. Our work, play, families and friends often ran parallel. His death will always frustrate me. We were going to get together that weekend after Thanksgiving.

I was raking leaves in my back yard when I got the phone call of his passing. The **remembrance** of that moment, as I recall it now, left me numb."

Tony Giving it His All

CHAPTER ELEVEN

GOIN' HOME

Goin' home, goin' home, I'm a goin' home
Quiet like, some still day, I'm jes goin' home
It's not far, jes' close by, through an open door
Work all done, care laid by, going to fear no more.

There are never any real "good" byes. Most of them are always sorrowful and sad. The only joy someone can obtain from a "goodbye" is when the person who has left returns home, back home to their loved ones, home to their families and friends, home to where the heart is. So sometimes saying "goodbye" leaves a bitter ember to the person left behind, either standing at the door, at the airport waving so-long, or worse yet leaning over the grave where you are left to inter your loved one.

It was not only the worst day *of **my** life*, but also for the many friends and family members who found it to be a most dreadful, painful day for them to have to say "goodbye" to someone so special.
From my thirteen year old Grandson Andrew, who felt a great need to express his feelings as follows:

Empty Spaces
Dedicated to my Uncle Tony

Uncle Tony, a man I knew little about
    Yet his death has destroyed my outlook on life.
I've been told so much, then I realized the pain
    his death caused my family.
When I saw the tears run down my mother's face.
Almost every day I think, how nice life would be
    with Uncle Tony back.
But we live in a world of so much pain and anger.
    So I guess, he bought his own Stairway to Heaven.
But we will always remember you, Uncle Tony
                Love Andrew Maurer

Mary and Frank Varlese, Tony's Aunt and Uncle shared their feelings in:

A Letter to my Nephew

"Dear Loving Nephew Tony:

When someone mentions your name it bring tears to our eyes and pain within our hearts. Yet, dear Tony we try to remember the positive things you shared in our lives.

We remember vividly that November day in 1997 when your father, somberly shaken and in tears, called us to inform us of their pain and broken hearts, we also felt lost. We did not know what to say except we cried and joined in sharing their pain. I told myself that when I would meet your parents, I would be strong. I told them 'we should mourn your passing but not to despair', at that very moment I repeated to myself, 'what am I saying?'. I embraced them and joined in their sorrow.

You know, dear Tony, that when your Aunt Mary and I come to visit at your new resting place I always ask you 'Why?', because we never have an answer that would console us.

I remember when you were a baby; together with your sister, cousins and other children you played with and had such a good time. Throughout the years, I watched you mature into an intelligent, funny adult. We were always so very proud of all your accomplishments.

We remember the holidays we always celebrated together. Especially recalling when you would ask your ZiZi Mary (Italian for Aunt) 'did you make your rum cake?' and she, of course, replied 'I certainly did, I made it just for ....all of us'. A loud hurray filled the air, especially from you. It was so good to see you laugh and be happy. I recall you asking Zi Zi Mary 'do you have extra tomato sauce?' We always served your favorite pasta (the homemade kind) with your extra tomato sauce. When the serving boat was placed on the table, again you had that great big grin.

I also recall one of the Fourth of July celebrations always held at your sister's house. You were in the pool with your baby son, holding him in your arms. When you came out of the water soaking wet you sprinkled water on your Grandma Grossa (on purpose, of course) because you always loved to tease your grandma. She, of course, yelled at you in a few well chosen Italian words including .... 'Questi cazze di guaglioni' (translated: these crazy kids). We all laughed, and then your grandma would turn her head towards me and smile. She would yell, but she loved your antics.

As you know, dear Tony, I had a few dreams of you recently, all with pleasant memories. The last dream I saw you coming out of our den, although I could not see your face clearly, you spoke to me; 'Zi Zi Frank! stop worrying, everything is OK, Everything is OK!' I have since no longer asked the question 'why?'

Dear loving nephew, until we meet again in God's own time, we will hold onto our loving memories. You are sorely missed and forever loved."

Uncle Frank and Aunt Mary

- - *- -

There is always the comeback when someone states or writes something very special for someone you love very much "of course your family misses and loved your son, he was part of the family, they *should* have loved him." This is such a sorrowful remark. I received such an avalanche of notes and letters from people who had known my son even for a brief encounter. He had a magnetism and exuberance of joy that he imparted to all he met, that they needed to let me know what an impact he left on **their** lives. Of course, his friends were the ones who knew him better than most and, of course, they wrote the more involved sentiments.

A Letter to Tony from Andrew Daniels

"Dear Tony,

Some of the most precious moments that as friends we shared will not translate into written words. They consist of private conversations, gestures, laughs and seemingly insignificant events and actions that made us friends.

I can never hope to write *everything* that comes to mind when I think of you. Different things that can happen each day will bring you to mind. Thoughts of joy and laughter.

If I was to list my own life's tragedies of losing my sister when I was five years old, my parents divorcing when I was six, my mother's passing when I was twenty-two, your death when I was thirty-seven is among them.

The laughter, fun, humor and warmth of our friendship will always be remembered and embraced. It is those good thoughts and memories that help me get through the tough days.

You are a good friend and I miss you."

Andy

The following was received from Ed Gelb, a close colleague, and a friend saddened at this loss.

October 2000

"Dear Tony,

If I could write to you now, here are *some* of the things I would say to you:

I knew you for about ten years through our mutually close friend, Andrew Daniels. I knew so much about you through Andy since he worked so closely with you at the accountant firm, Margolin, Winer and Evans. Through his continual conversation of your humor, laughter, and the goodness you enabled others to feel, I wanted to get to know you better. I found that when we started becoming closer that Andy had left out a really important part of *you.* You were so incredibly smart, sensitive and insightful in many ways.

I actually hoped and believed that one day we would work together and build a really successful firm. When I had mentioned it to you, you gave me the distinct feeling it could be possible. We had bounced the idea around a little bit and I don't know if you knew that I was completely serious. It was always a pleasure for me to be in your presence. You had not only humorous things to say but also other significant words with meaning. Tony, you had an aura of success as a person as well as in business. I look back and really enjoyed the short time that we spent together.

You have made me feel so many emotions that I realize how human I really am. I have to tell you that I miss you very much and wish that things could be different. I think of you and feel the joy of having known you, the sadness of your leaving us, the anger and frustration for not being able to do anything except think about you.

There were times you made me laugh so hard by your imitations of people, not maliciously but to stir a smile, the times we roared at the completely 'off the wall' statements you would make. One of the fondest thoughts that I have is when we all went away together on a golf outing and I couldn't believe how far you hit the ball at the same time you were truly laughing about something that struck you funny. I also enjoyed your dance routine at Andy Daniels' wedding. I couldn't believe at that time, you had the guts to act so wild with everyone watching and laughing at and with you. (Tony, I know you would do anything just to make people laugh).

I think of you all the time, as do so many other people. I know that you are fine and I want to thank you for being a friend to me.

Most lovingly, *Ed*

The following was received from:
My Godchild from Canada, Rosa Conte. She knew Tony
from a distance, but her sentiments to me in words of
comfort reflects such an inspiring message that I felt it
needed to be shared.

We Too Can Fly

We are all born to a world of change,
Though we may never know why.
We grow and learn, despair, rejoice, wonder,
 laugh and cry.
              ....and the days fly by.
Some of us look back with little regret or just a
wistful sigh, or worry our way towards the future.
And some of us even do our best to deny
              ....that the days fly by.
Each moment in time is a gift that comes and
              goes in the blink of an eye.
We question, as always, the meaning of life and
              the events that fill it, be they happy or sad.
              Sometimes there is just no reply to be had.
              So sorry I am that you flew away,
              though it was still not your time or day.
              So now all that remains
                    is for me to pray,
              Is that you lived life as well as it would
              allow.
              And that you knew you were loved so
              much   then
                    And it continues even now.
              To keep your spirit so near close by...
              ...Until the day when we too can fly.

- - * - -

The preceding letters were definitely written by family members and Tony's longtime friends, but the following note I received after his death was by someone who had just recently met him, possibly knew him only a few months, and at a time when Tony was not at his best and not his normal self.

"Dear Mrs. Varlese:

My note in memory of your loving son, a brother, a husband and a father. He was someone who meant many things to many people and who, even three years later, is still missed each and every day. When I met him I saw a son who brought joy and happiness to his parents. I know now he is a brother who will never be forgotten by his sister. A father to two wonderful boys who will grow up in his image.

Tony, your passing was too soon and did not give you the opportunity to make the impact you could have had on the world. You changed people's lives for the better and we thank you for those moments we still remember fondly. We miss you, yet are grateful for the time you spent with us on this earth. The years came and went far too fast but provided us with memories and the strength to continue in your memory. Seeing you leave this world was painful but we know you are in a happy place now. Tears still come to our eyes now that you are gone but when the tears dry a smile will linger on our face in remembrance of you."

- - *- -

Although the person who sent this beautiful sentiment did not mind that I print it, wishes to remain anonymous.

My son as a teenager and as a young adult was never a neat freak when it came to his room, his clothes, and his sports equipment. I am not sure what his tidiness habits were when he left my home and was living in his own home. The only positive thing I can state about Tony's neatness was a definite plus in his favor when it came to his files, paperwork, bank records and certainly anything that was related to his work. He was as different as night and day when making a comparison regarding picking up after himself and working with documents.

Due to his precise handling and saving of documents, I am very emotionally able to share Tony's goodbye note which he addressed to me. Keep in mind this was very intense and very painful, but Tony's words are so overwhelming and so meaningful and they represent the kind of person he really was, I wish to extend his beautiful thoughts to everyone. This summarizes who and what he truly believed in.

Tony's Goodbye

My Life at Thirty-Five

"I remember growing up with a great sense of community and family in Rosedale, Queens. I lived in a small neighborhood with many friends. We did "dopey" things but basically we were good natured and enjoyed doing things that boys do. As I grew older and moved into a suburban town, I desired knowledge and concentrated more on my academics, unfortunately I never felt the sense of community I had in that Queens neighborhood. I was a bit isolated with fewer friends and more distance. I always felt as if I had an emotional side based on feelings and an inner spirit, but how many of us actually ever expose it to the outside world.

You go through adolescence and feel a need for love or in many cases lust, but can't quite understand how it fits into a complicated world. You don't really have much responsibility so it is easy to say you love but don't know the burning desire until you have other complications in your life. I believe I was 20 when I first fell in love. She was someone I met at work and I knew she had all of the qualities that cultivate a pure and natural love, which is unconditional and hard to die. Unfortunately, I could never express myself to her and lived in despair every time I was around her and only dreamt of what we could be.

I never met anyone like that again until October 4, 1986. All of my relationships were based on shallow feelings and I guess I never knew how to put the love I felt inside into practice. I know I have so much love, compassion and emotion inside but had never found anyone I felt I could share it with. When I met her my life changed. I remember how I longed to talk to her, her mere presence brought me joy and contentment and how lucky I thought I was.

Somewhere inside I lost the ability to act with my emotions and became a product of my own environment. This is not to say that the feelings of love were not there or never manifested themselves. It is just that they coexisted with other things that you don't realize are unimportant. I also would like to believe that the loss was mutual because we were so much alike. Maybe one day in another world perhaps we can forget the past and fulfill each other.

People like to say you have to work at love. I think you just have to make it a priority. It is always there, it just exists with other things. When I woke up, it unfortunately was too late.

I guess I will always be burdened with another side but just as I allowed that other side to exist in the forefront for so long I must bring the love and devotion to the surface. It is amazing how much better you feel with one versus the other. Some people never learn the lesson I have, but then again some people don't need to. The only tragedy is that now that it is here I have no one to share it with and there may never be.

I will always live with the memory of who I was and may always wonder if that person still exists. Only I can know that the pain and suffering of losing someone you ever truly loved can lead you to thoughts of ending your own existence. Did she deserve my love? I'll never know; just as I will never know if I could have experienced the love and happiness with the first girl I also truly loved. You can go through most of your life searching and never finding , or you could have found and lost.

-145-

I'll never know which is better. In both cases there is great pain, but I believe the latter makes you a better person.

Someday I'll learn to forget. Maybe someone will come into my life and I can be the person I now have learned I am and want to be.

Somehow, I actually feel lucky that I possess the qualities that brings real love and happiness to others and I feel sad that I may have been amiss where it counted. When I am forgiven then I can move on. Oh! how I wish you could hear my words, 'I Love You' and truly understand what they mean when I say them."

- - *- -

The condemnation of himself that these words reflect is the desperation he was feeling. Knowing Tony the way I did, I can read between the lines as well. He was hurting so bad and blaming himself and saw no reparation. My worst regret is that I had no idea of what was going on until it was too late, but how does a mother interfere with decisions of a grown son and still stay neutral. How does a mother convince a thirty-five year old to seek professional help that could possibly get him through these dark hours, days and weeks.

Goodbye-Thanksgiving Day:

November 27, 1997, *the day I died.* It ended in terms of what one would consider normal existence. Tony ended his life for his own reasons and on his own terms. Yes, he did leave behind two young children and I can not tell you how many times the remarks were made to me, 'how come he did not think of his sons?' 'How could he do such a selfish thing". " How come he did not love you enough?" "Was he crazy?" " Why did he take such a permanent solution to a temporary problem?" Again, all these questions, they were logical ones and perhaps I would have made similar comments years ago when my life was perfect. Yes, I would have had compassion if a similar story were told to me. Yes, I would be sympathetic. Yes, I would say how sorry I was. "Yes, I can imagine what you must be going through". It always seemed it would be something a person could cope with. How wrong, how mistaken I was. There is nothing more devastating , nothing more tragic, nothing more incomprehensible, nothing more earth shattering, nothing more unbearable than the loss of a child, perhaps the loss of an *only* child. The death of your off-spring is bad enough but when the stigma is added, due to suicide, this loss becomes exacerbated.

As we did every year since I can remember, at least thirty years, Thanksgiving Day was celebrated at our home with as many relatives that could make it. Sometimes twenty, sometimes thirty. It didn't matter, there was always enough food for at least fifty. We experienced great joy from family gatherings, it didn't matter that it was a lot of work in the preparation of such a grandiose meal.   The memories, the joys we each and every one of us captured from these get-togethers are immeasurable.

The year 1997 was NOT to have one of these memorable days. Tony was already in a very upsetting and emotional, and a not so coherent, frame of mind. All he wanted to do was try to resolve his problems and bring back the situation to the way it used to be. He wanted so desperately to put his family back together again. This particular day he exerted extra effort in trying to accomplish this maneuver. He made arrangements with one of his clients in Manhattan that he would be taking his family to their office on Fifth Avenue to view the Macy's day parade from their windows. He also had paid reservations at a restaurant on Fifth Avenue to take his family to dinner after the parade was over. (The best laid plans of mice and men?)

It was not like Tony to disappoint us, but this was something he felt he had to do, something he *needed* to do. We all understood that Tony had to do something special *for* his family and *with* his family. We were disappointed, but we were happy that Tony was trying to make plans that would make his family happy and perhaps he would find some joy and peace in himself. The good of his marriage and the happiness of his sons were the important issues here, we would make other plans. Tony and I had confirmed plans that we would celebrate Thanksgiving on Friday, it didn't make a difference as long as we would be together. We were all very sad, but we fully understood the situation and so we accepted Tony's plans.

Tony called to inform us that there were changes in his plans. He reassured me over and over again he would be spending the next day, Friday, with us and reiterated that he was looking forward to having his favorite foods. Did I make his homemade pasta? Did I make his favorite escarole soup? Did I make the sausage stuffing he liked with all the other fixings a feast contains. I responded to all his inquiries and never once heard a quiver in his voice to indicate that something serious was going on. In fact, we spoke for several minutes, he was constantly reassuring me that everything would be okay. He made other plans with some friends to share the dinner reservation with them. He said he had put a $100 deposit to save the reservation and he did not want to waste the dinner and perhaps his friends would enjoy being treated. I **vigorously** argued with him and tried to change his mind, but to no avail. He had made up his mind and I wasn't going to change it. I pondered his decision and ultimately conceded; hoping maybe a change of scenery, a change of pace might do him some good. Perhaps being out of a family setting would cheer him up. I knew how much he loved to be with his family, but his family had left and he was left alone and did not want to burden us with his loneliness and sadness. I told him I understood, but deep down I did not , I was very sad about the situation and I knew I could not make it better.

A half hour passed and the phone rang again. This time Tony asked to speak to his father. I handed the phone to my husband and heard my husband repeat the same answers I had just given Tony. His dad questioned him if he was doing okay and not upset with the outcome of the planned day that did not materialize. My husband also questioned Tony about the remark "I think I will end it all", Tony's response to his dad was that he made the remark in an effort to spoil her day.

These were Tony's last words and what was really happening was that he was saying his "good byes" to us. His voice was not different, he was as jovial as he could be, he was as calm as anyone would imagine, he was not acting strange or saying anything to us that would lead us to believe that he was contemplating taking his life.

After we finished cooking and packed up the food which was about one hour later after the phone calls, we headed to our daughter's home for Thanksgiving dinner. On our way to her house we drove by Tony's new home, which was only three miles west of Gina's, and we were hoping he was still home and perhaps we could convince him to change his mind. We circled the street, his convertible was not in the driveway and we assumed he had already left for the city to meet up with his friends. When we arrived at Gina's house she recounted a phone call Tony made to her which repeated the same remarks he had made to us except that perhaps he would sleep over one of his friend's home instead of coming home to an empty lonely house.

During dinner, I was very upset that the day did not go as planned and I missed having Tony with us, for this was the first Thanksgiving dinner he had missed having with us in his whole life. We left Gina's house early because we all had a very sad quiet day. My husband and I drove by Tony's house again hoping to see his car in the driveway. This was not the case, and since there was no car we continued on home to Kings Park. I tried to call his home several times during the evening, there was no answer.

We all know marriages have their ups and downs, so Tony's was no different. **From his wife's recollection:**

"Tony was spoiled in many ways. I tried to give him ultimatums but I never followed through with any of the threats and never held him accountable. I have many regrets now (hindsight is always better than foresight), yet at that time I did not realize what Tony was going through. Only now I fully understand what Tony was feeling. Tony had become someone I did not know. The last few days of his life he did become more open, talked for hours, actually listened to what I had to say, sending jokes via e-mail. I did not really know who this man was now, but he reminded me a great deal of the person I met back in 1986, but hesitated to be sure. Only time would prove this change, but Tony never liked waiting for anything- traffic, long lines, etc. As mentioned previously, Tony was always on the fast track and that characteristic remained with him even during his depression. That characteristic, I know now, spelled disaster. Had I known then what I know now about suicide, I would have made sure Tony was never left alone. I look back and remember it all felt like I was watching a movie. Tony was rapidly losing weight, despite the fact that I was buying his favorite foods. He loved his mother's food but still ate nothing. He stayed home more and was with the boys more. He would even sleep with them at night. It was as though he was making up for lost time from the past, but now I feel he was making up for lost time in the future that he would be missing.

Tony told me several weeks before he took his life he had thought about taking his life and how he would do it. Sure, we all have moments when we wonder why should we keep going, life is tough but the fact that he even contemplated a plan made me concerned. I shared this with my marital therapist. I really wasn't sure if he was trying to manipulate me or not. My therapist gave me some names for Tony to seek help. He refused these names, but he volunteered to see *my* therapist. This, of course, upset me because I felt he would be interfering with my therapy. I also know Tony received names of other therapists from co-workers and friends, but again he refused. I never thought he was serious about his thoughts. My rational mind thought: 'Well, I guess he does not really want to take his life, if he did, I felt any person in their right mind *would* seek help!!!'. Only now, I realize how ignorant I was about suicide ideation.

The events of Thanksgiving Day, the day Tony took his life, went pretty much in sequence as written by his mother with the inclusion that the plans had changed due to weather conditions and the fact that he was out late the evening before and slept later than usual. Since the plans went awry Tony got angry, has face got tense and very gray. He stormed out of the house and returned around 9:00am. When he returned he told me he had just visited his grandmother's grave. He did not know what to do; he wanted to be with her. The look on Tony's face frightened me. He started telling the boys that he was a bad father and mommy was going to find them a new one. I got furious with him. I did not realize at that time I was dealing with a person whose mind had gotten so sick. When he told me he was going to take his life and that no one could stop him, I stood and wondered, 'Who was this man, this man who loved himself and life more than anything (or so I thought)'. I think I was in shock. I called his sister Gina and shared the events of the morning with her. Gina said 'I'll be right over'. Tony got really angry and took off again in his car. An hour later, Gina had just left our house, Tony returned home and said he was fine. He was very calm, so much more like he used to be. He even told me (I don't know if it is true or not) about an incident when he was twelve, after being bullied in school, he had taken some pills but never really intended to take his life and would never take his life. He asked me to leave because his mom and dad were coming over and they would be angry. I got ready to leave, I thought the worst was over and he would have the support he needed.

The continuing events evolved as previously written, except, as we were leaving I asked Tony to say good-bye to his sons. He came to the car and said good-bye, he told them that he loved them and to never forget him. After questioning Tony about this remark, he stated he meant for today, for it was the first Thanksgiving they would be apart. As I got stuck in traffic on the Throgs Neck Bridge I pondered returning home, but it felt safer to continue driving, for some reason.

I will always live with the what ifs. I think what if I called the police for intervention, and had him admitted to a hospital maybe he would be alive today. Or knowing Tony and his special way with people, he would convince the police that I should be the one needed to be committed. I know Tony did not want to die, but we were not dealing with Tony, we were dealing with a person who was severely depressed and was not rational. Much like dealing with a person who is on drugs, except, dealing with a person who is mentally and emotionally out of sync is harder to detect. In retrospect, I see all the signs for a suicidal person, but at the time I was too close to the situation to realize the outcome.

All I can do now is be a better person, use this experience and watch over his sons closely. I believe there is a greater plan that is beyond our understanding and tragedies happen even though we do not like them. Although I wish nothing more than Tony to still be alive today, I know his death was not in vain and someday I might fully comprehend why life unfolded the way it did.

I know this book was written not only so you may get to know Tony, but also by sharing his life and death perhaps others can gain insight as to what to look for in a similar struggle."

- - * - -

Tony had said his good byes and so quietly he had made room in his disorganized garage, moved the huge amount of boxes (the boxes were still packed from the move) to one side of the garage and drove his convertible into the garage and proceeded to say further "Good byes". Tony scribbled, in crayon, notes of love to us while he waited for the carbon monoxide to take effect.

I was transported to Stony Brook Hospital by ambulance when I collapsed after finding my precious son, the following day. To say I was not in this world would put it mildly. To say I wanted to die immediately myself is telling the truth of how I felt. Hospital personnel were very concerned about my emotional stability and so they issued a psychiatric consult. I was surely being guarded for my condition was serious and alarming.

I felt my son Tony was hovering over me and trying to console me but there were no words anyone could say to me that would make this real. I was indeed blessed that I had my closest friend and supervisor on call that day and so she was paged and arrived within minutes. Lisa Walters held my hand, held me in her arms and cried along with me for hours. She knew my son and could not believe what had happened. She did not leave my side all day, she waited for my family to arrive. They were entangled with police legalities and could not get to the hospital until later that evening. In addition to Lisa, Rev. Unger, the hospital Chaplain, also came to my assistance with words of comfort, with understanding and with prayers. Even with all this attention, I still wanted to die.

Black Tuesday - December 2, 1997

Numb from sedatives, garbed in black from head to toe, oblivious to anything or anyone within two feet away, I called upon my faith to convoke enough strength and courage to put one foot in front of the other, clutched my husband and son-in-law's arms and proceeded to attend my son's funeral.

The day itself was cold with what seemed like a slight ray of sunshine, but in my heart there was only darkness.

The mass of the resurrection concelebrated at St. Joseph's Church in Kings Park, the same church Tony had received his Confirmation and was accepted as a soldier of Christ. The same church where both his sons were initiated by the sacrament of Baptism, the same church Tony attended Sundays and holidays, especially "Easter". This was Tony's favorite of all church celebrations. He would spend the evening before and the entire night awake to observe the Easter Vigil. He would visit Kings Park Bluff overlooking the Long Island Sound and watch the sun rise. He truly believed in this resurrection of life, yet opted to deny himself of life itself. This is why sometimes I find it extremely difficult to comprehend the mechanisms which permit the behavior of someone so sensitive.

After the "Ave Maria" the eulogy was read by our niece Diana Varlese whom we felt would be the strongest, the most courageous, the one who could carry out this most sorrowful task. Yet , even she quivered and choked up several times during the reading.

The ride to Cavalry Cemetery in Queens was a total blur. The drugs, the tears, the pain, the shattering of so many lives was put to the test. How does one place a most cherished individual, six feet under the cold ground and think it possible that they could carry on? There is no answer to this rhetorical question, at least not for me.

While I attended a bereavement meeting, another bereaved mother stated that she attended her son's wake with poise, very staunch and completely composed "unlike the Italians who dress in black, sit in the first row in front of the coffin and proceed to cry out loud". I truly did not have to be Italian, all I needed to be was a "Mother" and I personally felt no other way to handle my grief. I dressed in black because I felt darkness throughout my entire being. I cried out loud because I could not find the courage to stifle my inner feelings. I cried a trillion tears for I could not control them. I sat is the first row because I needed to be as close to my son as possible, for as long as possible. I sat because there wasn't any strength for me to stand and I cried to try to ease some of the most excruciating pain any "Mother" would have under similar circumstances.

I was not upset or insulted when this statement was made, in fact I envied this woman for being so heroic and I wished I had her character to be so strong and be able to carry on as dignified as she did. Was her pain any less than mine, I doubt it. Each and every one of us is an individual with so many varied emotions, so we could not possibly handle the pain in the exact same manner.

I continued to dress in black clothing for an additional five months. Was I eccentric ? Maybe, but the fact that I was able to "dress" at all is what is significant. I could not have felt any differently no matter what color I wore, so what did it matter. To some people this is probably all nonsense, but I defy those same people who think my reactions were nonsensical to find themselves in my situation and losing a child, at any age, whom you love more than your own life and then respond to what sensible means in terms of emotional and physical pain. Someone also mentioned that logically I knew right from wrong, but since when is dealing with grief, logical.

Here I am three years later, can you spy me smiling? Sometimes. Do you see me laugh? Occasionally. Do I dress in lighter colors? When appropriate. At times I even sing, but only when it brings joy to others. Do I attend parties? If it is a necessity and obligatory. Is this the personality I had before Tony's death? No way. I used to be a very gregarious, out-going *people* person. Do I still care for and love people? You bet, but with all this sadness I have to contend with, it becomes very very difficult to be spontaneously joyous. Remember, I can not find joy in waking up in the morning simply because I can not share my joy with my son as I once did and then the thought of Tony missing out on the joy of life he would have had is extremely sad. The happiness he could have had is the reality I find so hard to deal with.

In Loving Memory of

Anthony Varlese Jr.

Entered Eternal Life on November 27, 1997
New Entombment October 13, 2001
Holy Sepulchre Cemetery, Coram, NY

You Are Here

A breeze flitters by, I stop to feel,
A chill sweeps through, I quickly kneel.
I sense this shiver so close, near by,
Is this his spirit that did not die?
A shadow, a trace of features sharp,
Engraved so deep within my heart.
That smile that glows from deep within,
Is this his spirit that has that grin?
The whisper sounds so dim, so still,
The tears now rush my eyes to fill.
His sighs I hear so clear, so loud,
Is this his spirit I feel right now?
A cloud takes shape, I see a form,
My mind plays games, I dare to mourn.
It may be our lives are far apart,
But I have Tony's spirit within my heart.

Love, Mom

Memorial WebSite@www.tonyvarlesejr.com

CHAPTER TWELVE

YOU'RE NOBODY TILL SOMEBODY LOVES YOU

You may be King, you may possess
the world and all its gold,
But gold won't bring you happiness
when you're growing old .

Our son did not want to die. He always had a joi de viere - a penchant for joy, love for life, a reason to see good in all things. Constantly and inevitably since Tony's death, I tried to read every note, every article, every story, every novel or non-fiction book regarding the taking of one's life, dying by suicide. The grasping at straws, the psychic readings, the unexplained phenomenon of thinking I could hear voices, seeing images that were not really there. The weirdness of the unknown, the stepping across the barriers, the crossing over, the bright light. You name it, I imagined and/or experienced it. The reality of death leaves a person numb, with no concept of time, place or existence.

Tony tried to hide his deepest inner feelings, except the fact that his love for all of us was the only true meaning of life for him that was evident. He felt guilty, he felt 'not in control', he felt abandoned, he felt he did not and could not have a future of 'normal' family existence. True, we were his family, myself, his dad, his sister and her family, but we were not his selected family.

On November 22, 1997, the last day I physically saw my son alive was at his niece Kerrin's 4th birthday. Tony was there with his son Anthony, who was having a great time playing with all the children under supervised party personnel. Tony's son was laughing, jumping, playing and having a real good time but all Tony could say was "Mom, I'm sorry". I questioned what he meant by that statement and so he sat down next to me and cried, "Mom, why do I feel like I don't belong here?. Mom, why am I not happy for you and your other grandchildren?". "Mom, why can't I pick up the pieces?" I quickly responded "surely you know that all this will pass, just give yourself some time, you know we all love you and will stand by you no matter what". Time will heal all things, so they say. Six days later we found our son a shattered man, desolate, cold, with tears on his cheeks, sitting slumped in his new convertible, in his new home, bought with so much *love*, completely lifeless. Here again, the phrase *love*, and so why did he not see it?

During the week of November 23rd, Tony called every day. One day he sorrowfully began to tell me: "Last night I had a bittersweet time with the kids. I wish I could forget her. I feel it is going to be hard being a father to my sons but I know I am giving it all I have and that should be enough. Mom was I that bad?" I quickly replied "Tony, you did your best, maybe it was not enough. Does it matter? Logic tells me it is her life and is entitled to her way, yes I know that eleven years of loving a person, no matter how badly you showed it, burns into your heart and all those memories into your head. I wish you could let go right now." I desperately tried to convince him he should not take all the blame and burden himself with all this guilt. Oh! how I wish I could have succeeded, it could have been so different.

Tony went on to say that everyone told him he would be okay, and quoted "I'll find someone, I'll have fun, I have a lot of things going for me. The problem is that those same feelings probably caused my arrogance so I shut them out. Sometimes I feel pretty pathetic but since when is my love and devotion something I should be ashamed of. I guess that is why I feel so much better when I talk about it because most people do sympathize. Mom, I know there are things I screwed up in my life and the sad part is every time I think of things to look forward to, it doesn't seem like there is much to anticipate. Believe it or not I am not ready to be single. I want to be married, but in the right way. I know I can make it right but I will have to wait."

Our conversations constantly included his remarks that "there are the boys. How easy it would be to get so wrapped up in making my life better, even temporarily, and forget about the kids. That would be okay if they were older and independent, but right now they need so much love and attention. I don't want to feel like a baby sitter either, but I can't force myself to be a father by always trying to plan their time."

Tony's attitude at that time was that nothing mattered any more. He was getting very impatient. He was not thinking of his happiness at all, it just didn't exist for now. Why was he not getting angry? There were times when he felt good to be alone, but this was always isolated. He sometimes even hoped things would get better and go back to the way it was, but when reality set in he would slip back into that darkness. Why could he not eat? He constantly came up with his inadequacies of being a good father, these were self-inflicted accusations. One time Tony said to me, "Mom, why don't I get comfort from you and dad even when I know you are always here? I guess I'll never know the answers to all these questions. I guess I'll have to pray for positive answers. Sometimes I really hate this house, but no matter where I am I doubt I'll feel any better."

He told me he was going to church, even seeking advice from God, to help him figure out what he would have to do, and why did he have to endure so much pain. He knew deep down the outside person he sometimes projected was not always the good person he was on the inside. "Who am I suppose to meet, if no one, then why am I here? I guess until I get some answers, I'll just have to muddle through."

Truthfully, I thought it would be better for him, that his wife have her independence. The best thing for all concerned is to have it over with so he could put his life in order. He felt he had no kind of life right now. I also thought his oldest son sensed his hurt and the lack of some relationship. I knew it was hard for the child to deal with Tony's pain, but that's the only thing Tony had so much of lately.

I should have been more astute when I realized Tony was going to church more frequently than usual and discussing conflicts with his inner self. He would state: "I feel good, I really feel at peace, but when I think of my situation I get a pit in my stomach. But it really doesn't matter what I think. All that matters is that everyone is happy in the end. I wish the pain would go away and I wish it would stop hurting . God, help and guide me in whatever I do." How ignorant I feel now that this statement did not trigger a signal.

Two nights before the fatal day, Tony called and confided:

"The hurt is still with me. The irony of this situation is incredible as I just finished my first load of laundry. Here I am home with the kids. I actually don't mind the domestic duties or the time with the kids, mom you know how much I love them. I just miss her company and love. I am still confused about this situation and don't know what to do. Last night the boys and I went bowling and we had a great time. I had a ton of fun just watching the kids having such a good time.   Maybe this is what I should cling to. I still have hope of a family life the way it should be, but I have to let go and I will. The sooner the better. God, help me through the next few months. God will tell me what to do in His own way. I guess I just have to listen really hard."

"Tony, we are praying for you and things will be brighter, God will help you. Please hang in there, you have so much going for you." This was my answer to him many times when we talked about his situation.

The following are things we learn as we grow up and hang onto when we are adults. They are the basis of life itself and Tony would proclaim their importance :

   Honesty - no matter what the event, being *true* to yourself even though it may cause pain to another, is the most important. It prevents barriers and breeds trust.

Relationship - The most important thing is to be together even when you can't think of something to do. Sharing each others' time is the greatest compatibility.

Devotion - Romance and love must be nurtured. It doesn't only exist in the beginning or on special occasions. You must always remind yourself and renew your love for one another so each day can be as good as the first. Never be afraid to show your feelings and don't give in to anger and frustration. Feelings can only be conquered by love and devotion. Letting out anger doesn't kill it. Overcoming it with feelings of love and happiness does.

In a final letter Tony wrote to God, he questioned:

Why Do I Cry?

As I sit here thinking of things to do that would bring me contentment, and reflect upon these last days, I try to understand the reasons why I cry. I only wish we all had the ability to understand and figure out true emotions. It seems to me that there is no greater sense of peace than to express a feeling of good even if it comes at the expense of great sorrow.

I cry because I didn't realize that the little things we do for each other are not done out of a sense of obligation but rather as an expression of undying feeling and compulsion.

I cry because I didn't understand that true love comes from togetherness. Whether talking, shopping, walking, watching a movie, being together and sharing time should bring the greatest joy and provide the greatest release.

I cry because I did not take the time to write or speak my true feelings but instead masked them with thoughts of anger.

I cry for not knowing that the greatest stress release is the joy of company.

I cry for not understanding that the person you are devoted to is always the most beautiful.

I cry for making excuses for not doing the things that meant the most. I know this now because the only comfort I have comes in the company of friends and family.

I cry because I didn't realize that the simplest things are always remembered and that the expression of feeling is not measured since it is the act that matters. We all need tokens of friendship and love. Whether they be simple cards during holidays or a compassionate phone call during tough times. I thank God for the compassion I have received from people these last few months.

Most of all, I cry because the person I have become can not make me the person I've been. Putting hollow functions ahead of time together is a destiny of loneliness.

- - * - -

Suicide is not to blame for my son's death. Circumstances beyond his control created a person he no longer knew or understood. Suicide ideation creates a dark black hole which whirlpools one into sinking deeper and deeper, until there is no longer even a slight chance for reaching out to ask for help.

Any death, but especially suicide leaves a barrage of questions for the survivors. How do we go on? There are no answers, only more questions. Why? How did this happen? Where was I when the desolation took hold? When did I become so blind I did not see the despair? Were there calls of help I did not hear? Again , the what ifs? The how come? The wheres? The whens and most of all the whys? Why him. Why me. Why us.

Understanding suicide with all the textbook illustrations, graphs and study cases can somehow bring a certain concept of it to light, but how much of the human psychology tracts a textbook presentation and how much can a lay person understand. Even if we did comprehend the mechanisms fully, can we really accept how a person we love so deeply could possibly hurt so badly and be inflicted with so much torment that they squeeze the breath out of their own life and then leave this same torture and pain to those left behind that I find myself praying for death; because I also find living without my son so unbearable and almost an impossibility. Does God want to hear my own pleas? Did God hear Tony's pleas? Was God listening then? Is God listening now? One day my grandson Andrew remarked to me "Grandma, God is listening, He does hear you, but right now He has to put you on hold". Words of wisdom from a thirteen year old. I am positive God knows my anguish, knows my pain and in His wisdom has other plans for me. Everyone's life is a thread of silk intertwined on a huge tapestry and while here on earth all we see are the knots on the back of the tapestry, each knot representing one life, and when we proceed to cross over and are positioned on the front side of the tapestry, only then will we be privileged to see the entire vision of what was meant to be and what we were called to do.

Suicide inevitably causes a domino effect and so the need for realization must be achieved. This residue of a family must be watched and guarded. The medical profession involved with the behavior of the psyche can possibly reach the patients already known to have psychological disorders, but where do survivors go? Whom do we turn to? Where do we seek knowledge and find out how to cope with the aftermath of suicide. The pain is incomprehensible and so we falter, we float into a make-believe existence, if an existence at all.

It seems in all my readings the element that is sometimes missing is the answer to "How can I go on?" Statistics note the issues of those suffering from manic depression, schizophrenia, those with family history of depression, bi-polar disorder, deficit attention disorder, even those affected by recorded subliminal messages that are aimed at the subconscious. The culprits are numerous. Every story is similar and different all at the same time, because the outcome is the same, the victim's reasoning is the same. The common denominator is that the person who died of suicide was in **extreme pain**. That cause never converts.

A person like my son, who could not face the future, could not see beyond his immediate pain, and I truly believe in his case and I am sure in hundred of other cases, the right help at the right time might have prevented his death. I feel his death possibly could have been averted with the proper intervention at the right time. I am not eluding myself, but who better than a mother who gave him birth, who taught him right from wrong, who taught him good things, who raised him into maturity, why did I not sense that his acute psychotic behavior was not just a temporary setback and that *time* was of the essence.

How a person decides to end his pain is somewhat insignificant, it may only serve to reassure that it truly was a suicide and not foul play or an accidental outcome.

The brain is a very complex mechanism, to try to justify one's action at any specific time truly would be an enormously involved psychoanalytical feat. We know of specific cases where suicide is completed while under psychiatric care in a hospital setting. Every human being reacts differently to any similar situation, to try to categorize someone's mental behavior seems insurmountable. Just think, how many married couples who get divorced (certainly thousands, statistics prove 50% of marriages end in divorce) find the need to end their life. The ratio of suicides to these divorces is minimal.

Tony was not manic depressive or so I thought, certainly not schizophrenic. From my conversations, he presented himself with undue guilt but yet continued to express so much love. At this point he was a shocked, disappointed man when his ideals were shattered, his personality was altered beyond compre-hension both to himself and others.

Statistics also rank of the long term mentally ill, so it is very far fetched to see a bright, normal hard working, decent, faithful husband and devoted father to go over the edge. He tried to salvage pieces, he tried to understand, he tried to cope, he tried to fit in. He, unbeknownst to his close family, did try to reach out for help but very obscurely. He found it difficult to let down his guard. To admit he was frail, hurting and downright sad was not the manly thing to do in his ungodly reasoning.

Those questions of why, over and over, time after time, what causes the pain and that horrible cycle of trying to carry on, either for the victim or for the survivor are the most frustrating. The realization that there is no going on, only faking an existence. For the survivor there is "A chain that has been broken, then repaired by solder, becomes a very thin bonding agent, the chain becomes very weak, it can hold but NOT very tightly. The original bond to that chain is missing and that is where the weakness lies."

To carry on, to go through, to move forward is the most challenging feat any one human being is forced to endure. There are prayers, there are the services, the rituals, the religious devotions, there is always the strong faith in God, and maybe someday the tapestry, when completed, will show the why and then the how we were to go on. Until then, our hearts will ache, our tears will not ebb.

The *sorrow* is not solely in the *dying*, but also in the *surviving*. We rationalize their pain, especially my son Tony who seems he needed to put it to rest because his love was so great, but at "What price Love?"

Recently, I heard a prophetic statement that "God did not promise us earthly happiness, what He did promise was Eternal Happiness with Him". I must believe this in my heart, and ***"Until We Meet Again Son, I will continue to Sing your Song"***.

The Afterglow

I'd like the memory of me to be a very happy one.

I'd like to leave an afterglow of smiles when every
day is done.

I'd like to leave an echo of whisperings down the
way.

Of happy times, laughing times and bright and
sunny days.

I'd like the tears of those who grieve to dry
before the ending sun.

Because of memories that I leave behind,
when every day is done.

Author Unknown

EPILOGUE

THE SILENT EPIDEMIC

Since my life as I once knew it ended on November 27, 1997, I am left with no other course of action but to try to put my last days and years to some useful existence, not for myself but for others. I need to "shout from every roof top" that suicide awareness should be a major concern for all Americans. Every fifteen minutes our country loses a dear one to suicide.

When I was made aware that my daughter's physical impairment may have been caused by the drug Bendectin, which was newly put on the market for morning sickness in 1956, we tried to sue the pharmaceutical manufacturer. Since the statutory law time frame had elapsed we were not successful in proving a valid case for ourselves. What we were successful in doing was help add value to an already existing class action suit, and after years of investigation the product was removed from the market. This success, I hope may have saved some other baby from experiencing what my daughter had been put through. It was a long battle but with perseverance, the ultimate goal was accomplished. There were no compensations for either myself or my daughter, only the thought that a baby was spared the pain and anguish associated with physical challenges.

I am now in a similar situation where I am compelled to scream, reach out and help educate the public that suicide is being perceived as a crime of selfishness and a cowardly act. Recently there was an episode on television on the new Crime Scene Investigation show where it was clearly stated "this death could not be a suicide because the victim had his glasses on and a suicide victim is selfish and cowardly he would have taken his glasses off". This is how the public envisions anyone who completes a suicide, as selfish and cowardly. What an erroneous statement and what a horrendous misconception of what suicide is all about.

"Suicide is a self-inflicted death", the dictionary description. This type of death occurs all over the world. Some countries even accept this as an act of valor, but this concept is purely cultural and certainly not perceived as such in our American culture. On the contrary, due to limited information sometimes suicide is perceived as an act solely involving the *severely* mentally ill. Upon exploration, we now know that in the United States suicide is reaching epidemic proportions. Suicide is still a leading cause of death worldwide, and it should be considered a public health problem because enough research has been accomplished to link suicidal behavior to numerous intricate complex causes. The most significant of these causes is "Depression".

From the recount of my son's short life, not only I but, all who knew him would emphatically state he was the most unselfish person you would wish to encounter and certainly not a severely mentally ill person. As far as being a coward, I think it takes a great deal of courage to actually go through with ending your life, whatever method is chosen. Just close your eyes and visualize not being able to open your eyes again. Do you really think you could continue? Your human instincts would be to open your eyes immediately. It is only because the suicide victim is NOT thinking clearly, if at all. The suicide victim sees only darkness anyway, there is no need to close their eyes, their eyes are already blinded by their pain. Their pain consists of physical, emotional and most of all mental pain. What the public refuses to accept is that this pain we are discussing isn't always a long chronic one, sometimes it is only a short lived pain but a crucial element in the process of contemplating and succeeding in taking one's life. Immediately the public's reaction is that the victim was a "terminal" manic depressive, a schizophrenic and any one of many long term mental disorders. True, a large number of suicide victims are the long term patients and yet a great majority of even those patients are helped and saved. The patients under psychiatric care are being cared for and watched. True, even some of those escape the vigilant watch and manage to carry out their self-destruction.

Yet, keep in mind there are numerous cases where the patient is helped with counseling and medication and that they *can* and *do* lead a fruitful life.

What is so essential is that the public should be made aware of the causes that preclude suicide afflict both those who have either long-term or short-term mental disorders. The public should be educated to the fact that suicide in some people *can* and *should* be prevented. If the stigma that suicide carries is eradicated then the public can confront the problem with openness, caring and compassion. So many have the concept "if you don't talk about it, it won't happen". If the subject could be approached without fear of the stigma that accompanies suicide then openness will lead to education and understanding of the subject and from that point help can be sought and intervention may be the crucial pivotal affect needed for prevention.

We have a serious problem not only with ourselves, the survivors, but with society itself. The concept the public conjures up is that the mentally ill are sometimes blamed for bringing on their own illnesses (i.e. drug abuse) or they are seen as someone whom fate has been unkind to. Perhaps this may be why most societies and the populous automatically stencil the stigma or a mark of shame onto the act of suicide. Research today has come a long way towards health education and improved areas of recognizing this serious illness and great strides are being made for the advocacy for the mentally ill.

We should always keep in mind when we are discussing "mental illness" that it involves a myriad of disorders. We deal with the more well known manic depressive, the schizophrenic and to this we can add people with panic disorder, phobias, manias of all sorts, eating disorders, post-traumatic stress disorder, Alzheimer's, anxiety, bipolar, personality disorder, cognitive disorder such as delirium and dementia, substance abuse disorder, impulse-control disorder. Just scanning these many disorders which reflect the complexity of the brain, we can certainly try to understand that mental illness is not solely reserved for one category. In our general society today and its correlation to suicide the most common of all mental disorders, is ***depression***, long-term or short-term.

In a conversation I had with a friend recently the subject of the correlation between mental illness and suicide arose and she became very indignant when I tried to explain that the person who completes suicide is not in his or her normal thinking behavior pattern. She refused to accept that the person she lost to suicide may have been due to any one of the disorders associated with 'mental illness'. Again, a misconception of mental illness. It certainly seems that the public accepts the fact that a person can experience an illness in every other part of the body, i.e. heart, liver, vascular, glandular or a number of other components but hesitates the thought that the brain can and may have a dysfunction. Some studies have also shown a ***genetic*** influence on how different people respond differently to similar situations. This evidence is not completely certified. This study is still on-going.

The brain is a very complex mechanism and any number of disturbances can effect its function. There are chemical substances that help the brain to communicate and most importantly helps regulate a person's emotions and behavior. Too much or too little of these chemical substances have been associated with depression. Research is also still on-going in this area of association with 'mental illness'.

As in all illnesses the first step is to seek professional help, why should mental illness be any different. Diagnosis is very complicated and should be handled by a recognized professional. At this point, self-help is not acceptable. Recognizing the symptoms, whether for yourself or someone you may suspect of uncharacteristic behavior, may be a saving solution. This is one way the public may be of service to themselves and others. The second step would be to accept the diagnosis and comply with necessary steps that are needed to comprehend this complicated illness. Our health professionals have made great strides in treating many of these disorders with drug therapy and psychotherapy. The treatment depends on the type and degree of severity of the disorder. Depression which is our most common and possibly the most understood of the disorders is perhaps the one that responds most successfully to treatment.

Depression in and of itself is certainly a major factor which creates the deterioration of the mechanism with which someone uses logic and reasoning in their behavior. In truth, mental illness is what sometimes the uneducated would automatically label the deficit to what is 'contrary to normal behavior'. What is normal behavior, and when is it not normal behavior? Is it before or after someone experiences a current physical illness, a trauma, a set-back or when someone is, afflicted with phobias, dementia, personality disorder, cognitive disorder or any one of the many disorders I have mentioned?

The most important step we all must take in handling this topic is to recognize the need to educate everyone to this type of illness. Our schools include sex education, AIDS education, drug addiction and health in general. We need to include MENTAL health as well. We need to explain feelings, normal or otherwise. We need to look at everyone as a unique person and perhaps recognize what may be perplexing to a certain individual. These efforts should be applied to every one, but especially in today's **stress** filled society, we need to emphasize our efforts on the young, the teenager, the ones who need the most guidance. Our schools *need* to include these basic educational elements and perhaps together with recognition, education and most of all public awareness, suicide may be prevented.

Let us all make an honest effort to bring this subject to the surface and maybe someday many of our most cherished, precious children will be saved from this '*silent epidemic.*'

Credits

Cover graphic by Karen Villano Silvestro

Precious Child   by Karen Taylor Good
    Chap. One

I Am Your Angel   by R. Kelly
    Chap. Two

Me and My Shadow   by Billy Rose
    Chap. Three

I Did it My Way   Frank Sinatra
    Chap. Four

Stairway to Heaven   by Led Zeppelin
    Chap. Five   Jimmy Page/Robert Plant

I Only Have Eyes for You   by Harry Warren
    Chap. Six   and Al Dubin

Tonight I Celebrate my Love for You   by Peabo Bryson
    Chap. Seven

You've Got a Friend   by Carole King
    Chap. Eight

He Ain't Heavy -He's My Brother   by Bobby Scott
    Chap. Nine   and Bob Russell

Memory   by Andrew Lloyd Webber
    Chap. Ten

Goin' Home   by Antonin Dvorak
    Chap. Eleven   and William Arms Fisher

You're Nobody Till Somebody Loves   by Russ Morgan
You   and Larry Stock/
    Chap. Twelve   James Cavanaugh

Printed in the United States
By Bookmasters